ClearRevise®

Edexcel GCSE
History 1HI0

Illustrated revision and practice

Option 11:
Medicine in Britain, c1250–present *and*
The British sector of the Western Front, 1914–18:
injuries, treatment and the trenches

Published by
PG Online Limited
The Old Coach House
35 Main Road
Tolpuddle
Dorset
DT2 7EW
United Kingdom

sales@pgonline.co.uk
www.clearrevise.com
www.pgonline.co.uk
2022

PG ONLINE

PREFACE

Absolute clarity! That's the aim.

This is everything you need to ace Paper 1 and beam with pride. Each topic is laid out in a beautifully illustrated format that is clear, approachable and as concise and simple as possible.

Each section of the specification is clearly indicated to help you cross-reference your revision. The checklist on the contents pages will help you keep track of what you have already worked through and what's left before the big day.

We have included worked exam-style questions with answers. There is also a set of exam-style questions at the end of each section for you to practise writing answers. You can check your answers against those given at the end of the book.

LEVELS OF LEARNING

Based on the degree to which you are able to truly understand a new topic, we recommend that you work in stages. Start by reading a short explanation of something, then try to recall what you've just read. This will have a limited effect if you stop there but it aids the next stage. Question everything. Write down your own summary and then complete and mark a related exam-style question. Cover up the answers if necessary but learn from them once you've seen them. Lastly, teach someone else. Explain the topic in a way that they can understand. Have a go at the different practice questions – they offer an insight into how and where marks are awarded.

Design and artwork: Jessica Webb / PG Online Ltd

First edition 2022   10 9 8 7 6 5 4 3 2 1
A catalogue entry for this book is available from the British Library
ISBN: 9781910523 44 5
Copyright © PG Online 2022
All rights reserved

Printed on FSC certified paper by Bell and Bain Ltd, Glasgow, UK.

THE SCIENCE OF REVISION

Illustrations and words

Research has shown that revising with words and pictures doubles the quality of responses by students.[1] This is known as 'dual-coding' because it provides two ways of fetching the information from our brain. The improvement in responses is particularly apparent in students when they are asked to apply their knowledge to different problems. Recall, application and judgement are all specifically and carefully assessed in public examination questions.

Retrieval of information

Retrieval practice encourages students to come up with answers to questions.[2] The closer the question is to one you might see in a real examination, the better. Also, the closer the environment in which a student revises is to the 'examination environment', the better. Students who had a test 2–7 days away did 30% better using retrieval practice than students who simply read, or repeatedly reread material. Students who were expected to teach the content to someone else after their revision period did better still.[3] What was found to be most interesting in other studies is that students using retrieval methods and testing for revision were also more resilient to the introduction of stress.[4]

Ebbinghaus' forgetting curve and spaced learning

Ebbinghaus' 140-year-old study examined the rate at which we forget things over time. The findings still hold true. However, the act of forgetting facts and techniques and relearning them is what cements them into the brain.[5] Spacing out revision is more effective than cramming – we know that, but students should also know that the space between revisiting material should vary depending on how far away the examination is. A cyclical approach is required. An examination 12 months away necessitates revisiting covered material about once a month. A test in 30 days should have topics revisited every 3 days – intervals of roughly a tenth of the time available.[6]

Summary

Students: the more tests and past questions you do, in an environment as close to examination conditions as possible, the better you are likely to perform on the day. If you prefer to listen to music while you revise, tunes without lyrics will be far less detrimental to your memory and retention. Silence is most effective.[5] If you choose to study with friends, choose carefully – effort is contagious.[7]

1. Mayer, R. E., & Anderson, R. B. (1991). Animations need narrations: An experimental test of dual-coding hypothesis. *Journal of Education Psychology*, (83)4, 484–490.

2. Roediger III, H. L., & Karpicke, J.D. (2006). Test-enhanced learning: Taking memory tests improves long-term retention. *Psychological Science*, 17(3), 249–255.

3. Nestojko, J., Bui, D., Kornell, N. & Bjork, E. (2014). Expecting to teach enhances learning and organisation of knowledge in free recall of text passages. *Memory and Cognition*, 42(7), 1038–1048.

4. Smith, A. M., Floerke, V. A., & Thomas, A. K. (2016) Retrieval practice protects memory against acute stress. *Science*, 354(6315), 1046–1048.

5. Perham, N., & Currie, H. (2014). Does listening to preferred music improve comprehension performance? *Applied Cognitive Psychology*, 28(2), 279–284.

6. Cepeda, N. J., Vul, E., Rohrer, D., Wixted, J. T. & Pashler, H. (2008). Spacing effects in learning a temporal ridgeline of optimal retention. *Psychological Science*, 19(11), 1095–1102.

7. Busch, B. & Watson, E. (2019), *The Science of Learning*, 1st ed. Routledge.

CONTENTS

Option 11   Medicine in Britain, c1250–present *and* The British sector of the Western Front, 1914–18: injuries, treatment and the trenches

Key topic 1   c1250–c1500: Medicine in medieval England

Key topic 2   c1500–c1700: The Medical Renaissance in England

Key topic 3   c1700–c1900: Medicine in 18th- and 19th-century Britain

Key topic 4   c1900–present: Medicine in modern Britain

MARK ALLOCATIONS

Green mark allocations[1] on answers to in-text questions through this guide help to indicate where marks are gained within the answers. A bracketed '1' e.g. [1] = one valid point worthy of a mark. There are often many more points to make than there are marks available so you have more opportunities to max out your answers than you may think.

Higher mark questions require extended responses. Marks are not given as the answers should be marked as a whole in accordance with the levels-based mark schemes on **pages 63-65**.

Understanding the specification reference tabs

This number refers to the key topic. In this example, *Medicine in medieval England*.

This number refers to the bullet point. In this example, *Rational explanations of the cause of disease*.

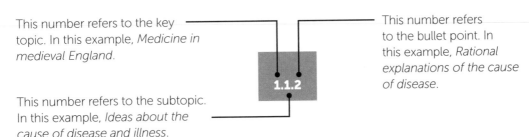

1.1.2

This number refers to the subtopic. In this example, *Ideas about the cause of disease and illness*.

THE EXAM

Paper 1 is split into two sections: Section A and Section B. The questions follow the same format every year, so make sure you're familiar with them before the big day.

Q1   Section A — 'Describe two features of...'

This question tests your knowledge of **key features and characteristics** of the period. There are four marks available and you'll be awarded one mark for each feature you identify, and a mark for each piece of supporting information you provide.

Q2 (a)   Section A — 'How useful are Sources A and B into an enquiry about...'

This question tests your ability to **evaluate two sources** and judge how useful they are for an **enquiry** (an historical investigation). The sources will be given in the exam, and you need to think about the sources' **provenance**: **when** the sources were created, **who** created them, **why** the sources were created and **what** the sources contain. You should evaluate the **usefulness** of the sources, as well as any **limitations** that they have, for example, a written source could be one-sided, or a photograph could have been posed. This question is worth 8 marks, and you need to evaluate both the sources to get top marks.

Q2 (b)   Section A — 'How could you follow up Source A to find out more about...'

This question tests your ability to **analyse and use sources**. You will be asked to follow up one of the sources from Q2 (a). You need to suggest: a detail you want to follow up, a question you want to ask, a type of source you could use to answer your question and a reason why you have chosen this type of source. Your answer booklet will provide sentence starters to help structure your answer. You will be awarded one mark for each valid point, up to a maximum of 4 marks.

Q3   Section B — 'Explain one way the ... was similar/different to...'

This question tests your ability to recognise **similarities or differences** between two historical time periods by using your **knowledge and understanding**. There are four marks available for this question. You will receive two marks for identifying a similarity or difference, and two further marks for providing specific supporting information.

Q4   Section B — 'Explain why...'

This question tests your understanding of **causation** (**why** something happened). You need to use your own knowledge, but there will be two stimulus points to help you. To get top marks, you need to include information that goes beyond these stimulus points. This question is worth 12 marks, so make sure your answer includes sufficient detail.

Q5 or 6   Section B — 'How far do you agree...'

For the final question, you'll have the choice of two questions but you only need to answer one. Both questions will give a statement, and you need to say how far you agree with it. There are 16 marks available for the content of your answer, and you need to demonstrate knowledge of **continuity, change and significance**. You'll be given two stimulus points, but you also need to include your own knowledge to secure top marks. Your answer needs to reach a judgement and it must be justified with supporting evidence. There are 4 additional marks available for spelling, punctuation and grammar, so make sure you carefully re-read your answer at the end and correct any errors clearly.

TOPICS FOR PAPER 1

Option 11:
Medicine in Britain, c1250–present *and*
The British sector of the Western Front

Information about Paper 1

Written exam: 1 hour 15 minutes
30% of total GCSE
52 marks (16 for Historic Environment, 36 for Thematic Study)

Specification coverage

Thematic study

Key topic 1: c1250–c1500: Medicine in medieval England

Key topic 2: c1500–c1700: The Medical Renaissance in England

Key topic 3: c1700–c1900: Medicine in eighteenth- and
nineteenth-century Britain

Key topic 4: c1900–present: Medicine in modern Britain

Historic Environment

Key topic 5: The British sector of the Western Front, 1914–18:
injuries, treatment and the trenches

Questions

The paper is divided into two sections:

Section A Historic Environment: One question that assesses knowledge and
a two-part question based on two sources.

Section B Thematic Study: Three questions that assess knowledge and
understanding. There are two options for the
third question.

SUPERNATURAL AND RELIGIOUS EXPLANATIONS OF THE CAUSE OF DISEASE, c1250–c1500

Most people in medieval England believed what the Church taught about the causes of disease. Supernatural explanations were common too.

Religious explanations

Disease is a punishment from God for people's sins.

God makes someone ill to test their faith in him.

Disease is God's way of cleansing our souls from sin.

The devil brings disease to try to make you turn away from God.

Supernatural explanations

Many people believed that **astrology** (the stars and planets) could cause disease. This was an old idea, but it became more widely accepted during c1250–c1500. Medieval doctors used **almanacs** (booklets showing the position of the stars and planets) to guide their diagnosis of the sick.

Some blamed Jewish people for causing illness until the Jewish population were forced to leave England in 1290. Others thought 'witches' cast spells to make someone ill or that evil spirits had invaded a patient's body. Exorcisms were performed to rid the patient of any evil spirits.

RATIONAL EXPLANATIONS OF THE CAUSE OF DISEASE, c1250–c1500

Rational explanations

Hippocrates

Many of Hippocrates' beliefs about how to stay healthy are still used today – regular exercise, healthy food, keeping clean and getting enough sleep.

Hippocrates was a doctor in Ancient Greece. He did not believe in religious or supernatural explanations. Instead, he thought there must be a **rational** explanation for disease and rational cures. His ideas were based on what he observed about illness. The Church approved of Hippocrates' teachings, so his teachings persisted for centuries.

The Theory of the Four Humours

Hippocrates developed the **Theory of the Four Humours**. He believed that:

- the human body contained **four humours**: blood, yellow bile, black bile and phlegm.
- each person had a different mix of these humours.
- when these humours became unbalanced, the person became ill.

| Blood | Yellow bile | Black bile | Phlegm |

Galen

Galen had been a doctor and surgeon in Ancient Rome. He developed Hippocrates' ideas and wrote a huge number of books. These included detailed diagrams of human anatomy that he had drawn when he carried out **dissections**. However, since Galen mainly dissected animals, a lot of his teachings about anatomy were wrong.

The books written by Hippocrates and Galen were the basis for medical training thousands of years later in the medieval period. Their ideas were thought to be universally correct, so it took a long time for their teachings to be challenged.

The miasma theory

The **miasma theory** was the idea that disease was carried by fumes or 'bad air'. It was an ancient idea that became increasingly widespread in medieval England and lasted into the 1800s. The Church approved of the miasma theory because they thought that being dirty and bad smells were a sign of sin, and this sin caused disease.

Factors for continuity

The dominance of the Church:
Most people didn't receive an education, so learning came from the Church which people visited every Sunday. Much of the population didn't question what the Church taught about illness.

Physicians (doctors) were trained at universities, but Oxford and Cambridge (the only universities) were run by the Church. Only books that agreed with the Church's ideas were available to students, such as the work of Galen and Hippocrates.

The Church wanted people to focus on living a good life in line with its teachings. It was suspicious of anything that could challenge its authority.

Dissections of human bodies were outlawed by the Church, so knowledge of anatomy came from dissections of animals and incorrectly applied to humans.

The acceptance of old ideas and lack of new ones:
Most people didn't look for new ideas because they thought the old ones were correct.

Scientific understanding and technology weren't advanced enough for people to find evidence or proof of new causes of disease.

Explain why there was little change in the understanding of the causes of disease c1250–c1500.

You **may** use the following in your answer:

- the Theory of the Four Humours
- the teachings of the Church

You **must** also use information of your own.

[12]

Your answer may include:

The Theory of the Four Humours:

- *The Theory of the Four Humours had been around since Ancient Greece, and most people accepted that it was correct, so they didn't look for alternative explanations.*
- *The Theory of the Four Humours was approved by the Church, so students training to be physicians at Church-run universities were taught that it was correct, and there was no need to look for alternative explanations for the causes of disease.*

The teachings of the Church:

- *Most people attended church every week, and they were taught that disease was caused by God as a punishment for people's sins. This meant that most people didn't look beyond God for an explanation for the causes of disease.*
- *Oxford and Cambridge were the only two universities which trained physicians, and they were run by the Church. This meant that physicians were only allowed access to books which were approved by the Church, such as Galen and Hippocrates.*
- *Human dissections were banned by the Church, so physicians could only rely on animal dissections to help them learn more about the body. This knowledge was often incorrectly applied to the human body.*
- *The Church did not want people to challenge its ideas or teachings.*

Other information:

- *The teachings of Hippocrates and Galen were thought to be correct, so no one challenged their ideas for centuries.*
- *Most of the population didn't have access to education, so they didn't question ideas about the causes of disease.*
- *Existing ideas, such as the miasma theory, seemed to make sense as people could see there was a link between dirt and disease.*
- *Even amongst the educated, there was limited advancements in science and technology, so there was little opportunity for people to learn and understand about the causes of disease.*

This question should be marked in accordance with the levels-based mark scheme on page 66.

Make sure your answer to this question is in paragraphs and full sentences. Bullet points have been used in this example answer to suggest some information you could include.

To get top marks you need to include information other than the bullet points in the question.

APPROACHES TO PREVENTION AND TREATMENT, c1250–c1500

Treatments were related to what people thought had caused disease.

Religious actions

Preventions

Going to church

Praying and fasting

Not committing sins

Flagellation – whipping yourself so God wouldn't punish you

Treatments

Going on pilgrimage

Praying and fasting

Touching holy relics

Giving offerings (money or objects) to the Church

Rational actions

Bloodletting (using leeches or cutting veins) and **purging** (making someone sick or go to the toilet) were believed to balance the four humours, and both were used to prevent and treat disease. Bloodletting could weaken the patient if too much blood was lost.

Galen's **Theory of Opposites** was another treatment based on balancing the humours. Patients would be given something 'opposite' to their symptoms. For example, if someone had a fever, they should eat and drink cool things, such as cucumber, to try to cool them down.

Most people knew that washing regularly, eating well, taking exercise and getting enough rest were all effective ways of staying healthy and preventing disease.

Keeping places clean and sweet smelling were thought to **purify the air** and keep miasma away.

The use of remedies

Many herbs and plants were used to treat disease in medieval times. People mixed homemade **remedies** that could be drunk, eaten, sniffed or bathed in. Creams were made to be applied to the skin. Some worked and are still used today, for example, willow tree bark is a natural pain reliever.

Food and drink were used as treatments. Some were effective, for example, wounds were cleaned with wine which helped prevent infection.

Other remedies were supernatural, for example, rubbing live or dead animals on wounds or burns.

People with the same illness could be given completely different treatments. It was believed that factors specific to an individual caused their illness.

THE ROLE OF THE PHYSICIAN, APOTHECARY AND BARBER SURGEON

Many ill people were cared for at home by relatives or a local wise woman, but sometimes patients would be treated by a 'professional'.

Physician

There were very few **physicians**. Physicians spent 7–10 years at university and had to pass exams before they could treat patients. Training was based on reading books, rather than practical experience. They usually visited patients in their own homes, but were very expensive so only the rich could afford them. Physicians:

- diagnosed patients by examining their symptoms, urine and blood.
- compared urine to urine charts to assess its appearance, smell and taste.
- prescribed treatments and when they should be given.
- rarely treated patients themselves.

Apothecary

Most towns and some villages had **apothecaries** (people who mixed and sold remedies), so they were the most accessible form of healthcare for the average person. They were trained by other apothecaries and used recipe books of remedies, some of which were very old. Patients usually visited the apothecary's shop or home where they:

- mixed remedies (see **page 5**) for illnesses and ailments.
- sometimes diagnosed problems and gave advice on treatment.
- sold charms and other 'cures' for disease.

Barber surgeon

Barber surgeons learned 'on the job'. Some were highly skilled and experienced, but most were not. People visited a barber surgeon's shop for:

- cutting hair and shaving beards.
- bloodletting and pulling out rotten teeth.
- surgery such as amputating limbs.

Explain **one** way that treatment in the years c1250–c1500 is similar to the years c1900–present. [4]

In c1250–c1500, most people were treated in their homes by a family member.[1] People mixed their own remedies but also bought them from an apothecary.[1] This is similar to the present. When people become ill, they are usually looked after at home.[1] They use medicines bought from a chemist, in the same way that someone in the medieval period bought remedies from apothecaries to treat their illness at home.[1]

For more information about medicine in the years 1900–present, turn to **pages 30–40**.

NEW AND TRADITIONAL APPROACHES TO HOSPITAL CARE IN THE 13TH CENTURY

Many hospitals were in monasteries. Christians believed that it was their duty to care for the sick.

Hospital patients

Hospitals were initially places where poor or weary travellers could stay, often people who were on a religious pilgrimage.

However, more specialised hospitals emerged which offered care to people in the community. These included:

- Leper houses for leprosy sufferers (a disease which causes growths or discolouration on the skin).
- **Almshouses** for the elderly who could no longer look after themselves.
- Common hospitals which cared for the short-term sick.

The role of hospitals

Since hospitals placed a strong emphasis on religion, patients took part in regular worship, and monks and nuns would pray for them. The focus was on treating the soul not the body.

Physical care was done by older women, usually nuns, who had limited medical knowledge. However, patients sometimes got better as they had plenty of rest, fresh food and water, and hospitals were often cleaner than the average person's home.

Some hospitals were funded by charity, and some by the Church. Most were very small, although St Leonard's hospital in York had over 200 beds.

Hospitals increased in number during this period. There were around 1,300 by c1500.

St Bartholomew's Hospital – London

The name 'hospital' was given to these places because they offered hospitality.

'Medical treatment and care c1250–c1500 were largely ineffective.'

How far do you agree? Explain your answer.

You **may** use the following in your answer:

- bloodletting and purging
- the use of remedies

You **must** also use information of your own.   [16 for content + 4 for SPaG = 20]

Your answer may include:

Agree

- *Bloodletting and purging were used to balance the four humours. We know now that these treatments were ineffective, as imbalanced humours are not a cause of disease. Bloodletting was potentially dangerous as it could weaken the patient.*
- *Remedies could be prescribed and made by an apothecary or could be made at home. Many of these remedies were probably ineffective, such as rubbing a dead animal on a wound.*
- *Galen's theory of opposites, where a patient was given food or drink opposite to their symptoms, was a treatment based on balancing the four humours. Since we now know that an imbalance of humours doesn't cause disease, this treatment was ineffective.*
- *Since many people thought that illness was caused by God, a lot of medical treatments were based in religion. For example, people would pray to God or touch relics. Religious treatments were rarely effective.*
- *Hospitals run by monasteries were places where the elderly and the sick could receive care. A lot of the caregivers were untrained monks and nuns who treated a person's soul, rather than their body, so the treatments they gave, such as praying for the sick, were often ineffective.*

Disagree

- *Some remedies may have worked, for example willow bark contained natural pain relievers and wine could clean wounds.*
- *Inhaling miasma was thought to cause disease so one way of preventing and treating disease was to keep yourself clean. Although we know now that miasma is not a cause of disease, staying clean would have been effective for better health.*
- *Hospitals tended to be clean places where people could rest and get food and water, which could help people get better.*

This question should be marked in accordance with the levels-based mark scheme on page 67.

To get top marks, you must refer to the question and make a judgement on the statement, having outlined the different sides of the argument. You also need to include information other than the bullet points from the question.

Make sure your answer to this question is in paragraphs and full sentences. Bullet points have been used in this example answer to suggest some information you could include.

CASE STUDY
THE BLACK DEATH (1348–49)

The Black Death reached England in 1348 and spread across the country. Over the course of two years, approximately one third of England's population died.

Symptoms of the Black Death

The Black Death was the name given to a pandemic of **bubonic plague** and **pneumonic** plague. Bubonic plague was spread by the bites of fleas and caused **buboes** (swellings) in the groin and armpits, fever, vomiting and diarrhoea. Death usually came after 3–5 days, though 20% of sufferers survived. Pneumonic plague was spread via coughs and sneezes and caused respiratory issues, including coughing up blood.

Approaches to prevention and treatment

Religious

People believed the Black Death was a punishment from God, so they confessed their sins and asked for forgiveness through prayer. If a plague victim died, it was seen as God's will. Pilgrimages, fasting and **flagellation** (whipping) were all used to try to prevent infection.

Rational

Some believed that impure air – miasma – was responsible, so people attempted to purify the air by using strong-smelling herbs like aloe and myrrh, lighting bonfires and boiling vinegar. People fled or avoided infected areas, homes and people. Physicians advised bleeding and purging, or lancing (bursting) buboes. People were told to avoid baths as they believed they opened the skin to miasma.

Supernatural

Some thought the Black Death was caused by strangers or witches. Anyone considered a witch was driven away, and people wore lucky charms to keep themselves safe.

Government action

Local governments tried to enforce quarantines and ban large gatherings, but people didn't take much notice. Some local authorities stopped street cleaning to allow the stench to drive away miasma. However, King Edward III ordered more street cleaning in London.

CONTINUITY AND CHANGE IN EXPLANATIONS OF THE CAUSE OF DISEASE, c1500–c1700

1500–1700 was the time of the **renaissance**. People questioned old ideas and took a more **scientific** approach to understanding and diagnosing illness.

> The renaissance was a period in history where people across Europe began to take more of an interest in art, literature and science.

Change and continuity

By 1700, fewer people believed in supernatural or religious causes of disease and the idea that astrology caused disease also declined. By the end of the period few physicians believed the **Theory of the Four Humours**, although many ordinary people still did.

The idea that disease was caused by **miasma** remained popular but there were several new **rational** ideas based on the belief that disease was caused by something getting into the body such as '**animalcules**' (tiny animals seen under microscopes, i.e. bacteria).

Factors for change

- The **Reformation** (see below) meant the Church had less control over ideas, books and learning.
- The introduction of the **printing press** meant ideas reached more people quicker than before.
- Scientific enquiry and challenging someone else's ideas were more accepted thanks to the **Royal Society** (see page 11).
- Experiments with lenses led to the invention of simple **microscopes** in the 17th century. This allowed people to see tiny animals for the very first time, which led to the belief that they might have something to do with disease, but this couldn't be proven yet.

Factors for continuity

- People were slow to accept new ideas, and most people could not read new ideas for themselves.
- None of the new ideas had been proven – they were still just 'ideas'.

> The Reformation happened in the 16th century. King Henry VIII and the Church of England broke away from the Roman Catholic Church, so the Catholic Church had less influence in England. One of the features of the Reformation was the dissolution (closing) of the monasteries which impacted hospital care.

A scientific approach

Some physicians began to challenge old ideas. **Thomas Sydenham** (1624–1689) became known as 'the English Hippocrates' due to his impact on medicine after the 1660s. Sydenham was influenced by the work of **Vesalius** (see **page 15**) and **Harvey** (see **page 16**).

He used a more scientific, practical approach and diagnosed patients by observing their symptoms rather than using books, astrology and urine charts. He recorded patients' symptoms, their treatments and progress. He helped disprove that disease was caused by factors unique to a person – he treated the disease, rather than symptoms.

The influence of the printing press

The development of the **printing press** from 1470 onwards meant that books could be reproduced in a few days rather than taking months to copy by hand. This meant that new ideas could reach more people far quicker than before. It also meant that there were more books available, so doctors could have their own copies of important medical texts.

Most people were illiterate and couldn't afford books, so the increased availability and variety of books mainly impacted wealthy and educated people during this period.

Sydenham wrote books and articles, including 'Observationes Medicae' ('Medical Observations'), which were widely published until 1844.

The work of the Royal Society

From 1645, a small group of scientists began meeting weekly in London to discuss new ideas and discoveries. They built a laboratory with scientific equipment that members of the group could use, and began publishing books. King Charles II became interested and started going to meetings and viewing experiments, and from 1662, it was called the **Royal Society**.

The Royal Society had a big impact on communicating medical ideas:

- Sharing and challenging scientific ideas became more common, helped by Charles II's interest.
- It paid scientists to carry out experiments and then reported on their results, such as Leeuwenhoek's report on 'animalcules' in 1683. Leeuwenhoek had discovered bacteria, but it would take centuries for this discovery to have an impact on medicine.
- Its journal – *Philosophical Transactions* – helped spread new findings and invited others to challenge or build on them.

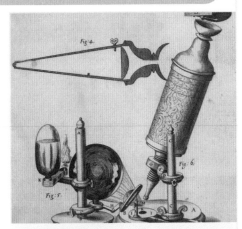

An engraving of an early microscope developed by Robert Hooke, a member of the Royal Society, in the 1660s.

Explain why new ideas about disease increased in the years c1500–c1700.

You **may** use the following in your answer:

- the declining influence of the Church
- the Royal Society

You **must** also use information of your own. [12]

Your answer may include:

The declining influence of the Church:

- *Due to the English Reformation, the Church lost a lot of influence during this period. This meant that the Church didn't have as much control over what physicians were taught.*
- *Scientists were able to challenge centuries-old beliefs about the causes of disease, such as the work of Hippocrates and Galen, which had previously been protected by the Church.*

The Royal Society:

- *The Royal Society encouraged the scientific community in London by giving members access to laboratories and scientific equipment.*
- *It also funded experiments, such as Leeuwenhoek's research on animalcules, which gave scientists more opportunities to make discoveries.*
- *It was supported by King Charles II. This gave it more authority and respect.*
- *The Royal Society's journal, Philosophical Transactions, spread new ideas and encouraged other scientists to challenge them.*

Other information:

- *Thomas Sydenham introduced a more scientific approach to diagnosing illness which was based on observing his patients' symptoms and recording how they responded to treatment.*
- *The introduction of the printing press meant that books could be reproduced much more quickly which increased the number of books available during this time. This meant that scientific ideas could be spread much more rapidly, more people had access to books and scientists were able to build on each other's work.*
- *There were advancements in technology, for example, the microscope. Better equipment meant that there was more progress in discovering ideas about disease.*
- *During the renaissance, there was a greater interest in scientific ideas across Europe, so there were more new ideas being shared.*

This question should be marked in accordance with the levels-based mark scheme on page 66.

Make sure your answer to this question is in paragraphs and full sentences. Bullet points have been used in this example answer to suggest some information you could include.

To get top marks, you need to include information other than the bullet points in the question.

CONTINUITY IN APPROACHES TO PREVENTION, TREATMENT, AND CARE, c1500–c1700

Despite the new ideas and discoveries of the medical renaissance, ways of preventing and treating disease largely stayed the same.

Continuity in care in the community and hospitals

As in medieval times, most people were treated in their own homes by a family member or local wise woman. Patients could still be treated by apothecaries, barber surgeons and, for those who could afford it, physicians. In the hospitals that remained following the dissolution of the monasteries (see **page 10**), patients were still looked after by people without formal medical training – mostly monks and nuns, though physicians were more involved.

Continuity in prevention and treatment

Prayer and fasting remained common ways to prevent and treat disease. Some still wore lucky charms.

Herbal remedies remained the most popular treatment. The printing press meant more people had access to books about remedies and how to mix them.

Bleeding and purging were still performed to keep people healthy as well as treat people when they were ill.

Keeping clean and sweet smelling were still thought to prevent miasma. Street cleaning was done more regularly.

Royal touch ceremonies (where the touch of a monarch was thought to cure disease) were popular throughout 1500–1700 but peaked during Charles II's reign.

A drawing showing Queen Mary I touching someone suffering from scrofula (a skin disease). It was widely believed a monarch's touch cured the disease.

Factors for continuity

New ideas about the cause of disease or new knowledge and discoveries by people such as Vesalius (see **page 15**) and Harvey (see **page 16**), took a long time to be accepted.

There were big steps forwards in knowledge of **anatomy** and how the body worked but these didn't directly impact on treatments or ways of preventing disease.

CHANGE IN CARE AND TREATMENT, c1500–c1700

There were some improvements to care and treatment during the renaissance.

The period 1500–1700 saw an increase in **exploration**. New discoveries from overseas, such as tobacco, were believed to cure many illnesses and ailments. Some of these discoveries worked, such as bark from the cinchona tree (a source of quinine) to treat malaria.

Quack (untrained) **doctors** were extremely popular. They sold a variety of treatments, but most did not work, and some caused harm, even death.

The science of **alchemy** (turning base metal into other metals) was also popular and led to chemicals being used as medicines.

A quack doctor from the 17th century.

Here you may be Cured

Hospital care

Many hospitals were closed in the late 1530s due to the **dissolution of the monasteries**. A few were taken over by local councils or charities.

As the number of monks and nuns in England dramatically decreased, care in remaining hospitals was mostly done by women as untrained nurses and helpers.

More hospitals had opened by 1700 but there were still nowhere near as many as in 1500. Physicians ran the new hospitals, and most hospitals employed surgeons and apothecaries but most of the people who cared for the sick in hospitals were not medically trained. Prayer was still a popular treatment, but trying to treat people using practical methods became the focus.

Around 625 monastic communities were dissolved by Henry VIII. This left many hospitals without any funding or people to run them, so they closed.

Improvements in medical training

By 1700, surgeons and apothecaries could only work if they had a licence from a professional body, such as **The Worshipful Society of Apothecaries**. To get a licence, they needed to complete training as **apprentices** to a master.

Professional bodies also checked the work of licensed surgeons and apothecaries by carrying out inspections of shops, the services they offered and the remedies they sold. This helped to regulate apothecaries and legitimise those who were highly trained.

The Worshipful Society of Apothecaries was founded by Royal Charter in 1617.

Physicians

By 1700, physicians' training was still largely based on books but thanks to new research, physicians had a better understanding of the human body (see below for Vesalius and **page 16** for Harvey).

Oxford and Cambridge remained the only universities in England, but they were no longer run by the Church.

The **College of Physicians** was opened in London in 1518. It issued licenses to physicians who had passed its exams (after completing training at university). Members of the college could meet and pass on knowledge.

Training was beginning to include practical experience. For example, St Bartholomew's Hospital, London helped to train physicians. **Dissections** were now legal, and more physicians carried out dissections themselves.

A scientific approach (see **page 11**) became more common and physicians (in training and after they qualified) began questioning and experimenting for themselves.

A physician writes a prescription, c1700.

The influence of the work of Vesalius

Vesalius was born in Brussels but studied medicine in Paris before qualifying in Padua, Italy in 1537. He believed in the importance of understanding human **anatomy** for medicine and surgery.

He carried out his own dissections on human bodies, especially after a judge gave him the bodies of executed criminals from 1539. He used a scientific approach to his dissections – recording findings using charts and diagrams, repeating his work and comparing many different bodies. He became Chair of Surgery and Anatomy at the University of Padua and taught many students.

Vesalius' book, *On the Fabric of the Human Body*, was published all over Europe in 1543. This ensured many people, including physicians, gained a better understanding of anatomy.

Vesalius was heavily criticised during his lifetime, and it took time for his work to be accepted, but his work inspired others to carry out dissections and experiment for themselves. For example, his student Fabricius would go on to teach William Harvey (see **page 16**) who made further discoveries about anatomy.

A modern version of a 1540 engraving of Andreas Vesalius (1514–64) with a dissected arm.

CASE STUDY WILLIAM HARVEY

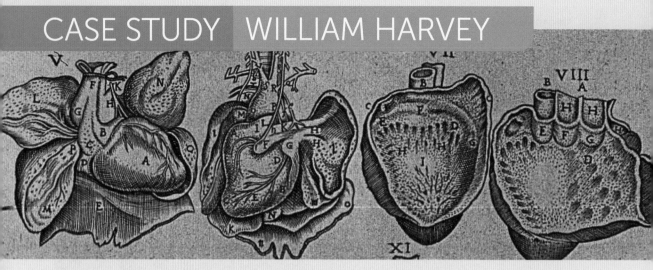

Harvey's (1578–1657) work improved knowledge of **physiology** (how the human body works) but, like Vesalius, it took time for his work to be accepted.

The discovery of the circulation of the blood

Harvey studied to become a physician at Cambridge University before continuing his studies in Padua. On his return to England, he lectured at the College of Physicians where he carried out public dissections. He taught students to observe their patients, rather than relying on books.

Harvey was interested in Vesalius' theories about blood which were different from Galen's. Experimenting with dissected bodies and live ones, Harvey discovered that:

- Blood from veins can only flow towards the heart and blood from arteries can only flow away from the heart but they are linked together in one system.
- The heart acts as a pump that circulates blood around the body.
- Veins and arteries only carry blood.
- Blood was not created by the liver as people had previously thought.

The impact of Harvey

Harvey published *An Anatomical Account of the Motion of the Heart and Blood in Animals* in 1628. His ideas shocked people and took time to be accepted (it was nearly 50 years before they were first taught in medical schools) but once they did, they had a lasting impact. He had disproved more of Galen's ideas, and he helped demonstrate that scientific methods and dissection were essential to discovering how the body worked. Others built on his work and made further discoveries.

Factors that helped Harvey

Harvey was taught by a student of **Vesalius** in Padua, so he learned from Vesalius' ideas and copied his methods. He was a physician for King James I and then Charles I – this helped spread his ideas and meant that more people took his ideas seriously. New technology, such as water pumps used to put out fires, inspired Harvey to think that the heart might work in the same way. Dissections had become legal in Britain and more physicians were carrying them out.

CASE STUDY
THE GREAT PLAGUE IN LONDON (1665)

The Great Plague of 1665 was the most significant outbreak of the plague since the Black Death. It was spread by bacteria carried by fleas, and killed about 100,000 people just in London.

Approaches to prevention and treatment

Rational beliefs and treatments

People still believed that plague was caused by **miasma**, so they lit bonfires and burnt tar. People carried herbs under their nose, hung them in their houses, or smoked tobacco to drive away miasma. Street cleaning increased.

Wealthy people, along with trained physicians, fled towns and cities. Ordinary people had to rely on plague doctors and quacks for treatment, which included rubbing buboes on to a bird in the hope of transferring the disease.

People were aware that the plague could be passed from person to person, so some stayed indoors and avoided people. They thought that the plague could be spread by touching an infected person's coins, so money was washed in a jar of vinegar.

Supernatural beliefs and treatments

The idea that the plague was caused by God, or the planets, persisted. People continued to pray and wear lucky charms.

The action of local councils

Councils took action to prevent the plague from spreading. The houses of plague victims were marked with a red cross and boarded up for 40 days. The councils employed **watchers** to monitor plague homes to make sure people didn't leave. Theatres were shut to prevent large gatherings, and local councils ordered stray animals to be killed. The border with Scotland was closed and trade between London and other towns was banned.

People fleeing urban areas contributed to the plague spreading across the country.

Killing stray animals meant that flea-infested rats spread the plague more easily without cats to catch them.

'The work of Vesalius was the most important development in medicine during c1500–c1700.'

How far do you agree? Explain your answer.

You **may** use the following in your answer:

- the work of William Harvey
- the development of the microscope

You **must** also use information of your own.   [16 for content + 4 for SPaG = 20]

Your answer may include:

Agree

- *Vesalius carried out dissections on human bodies. Prior to Vesalius, most knowledge of anatomy came from animal dissections, which were then incorrectly applied to humans.*
- *Vesalius' 'On the Fabric of the Human Body' was printed and distributed across Europe. This allowed other people to gain a better understanding of how the human body worked.*
- *Vesalius also used a scientific approach to his work. He recorded his work accurately and compared his findings across many different bodies. His work influenced others, e.g. Harvey.*

Disagree

- *Vesalius was criticised during his lifetime, and it took a while for his ideas to be accepted. His work on anatomy had little impact on the causes and treatment of disease.*
- *Practising medicine was better regulated in this period. For example, surgeons and apothecaries needed to receive training to be granted a licence.*
- *The English Reformation meant that the Church lost influence which allowed developments in medicine, for example dissections became legal, and scientists were able to challenge the work of Galen and Hippocrates.*
- *Harvey discovered that blood was pumped around the body by the heart. He published his findings in 'An Anatomical Account' which had a lasting impact on medical teaching.*
- *Like Vesalius, it took a while for Harvey's ideas to be accepted, although Harvey was a doctor for King James I and Charles I, so his ideas were more respected in England.*
- *Harvey's ideas helped people to understand more about the human body, but they didn't help discover causes and treatments for disease.*
- *The invention of the microscope in the early 17th century led to the discovery of tiny 'animalcules'. People thought that these tiny particles could cause disease, but it would take centuries for this discovery to be proven and to have an impact on medicine.*

This question should be marked in accordance with the levels-based mark scheme on page 67.

To get top marks, you must refer back to the question and make a judgement on the statement, having outlined the different sides of the argument. Remember to include information other than the bullet points in the question.

Make sure your answer to this question is in paragraphs and full sentences. Bullet points have been used in this example answer to suggest some information you could include.

CONTINUITY AND CHANGE IN EXPLANATIONS OF THE CAUSE OF DISEASE, c1700–c1900

In the 18th century, there were few new ideas about the cause of disease. However, the 19th century saw real breakthroughs in understanding.

Continuity in ideas 1700–1850

Most of the old ideas about what caused disease continued. The **miasma** theory was the most popular, but some still believed in the **Theory of the Four Humours**. Far fewer now believed in supernatural reasons or that God made people ill (see **page 2**).

New ideas 1800–1850

The early 19th century saw the development of the **Theory of Spontaneous Generation**:
- Tiny organisms (microbes) could now be seen on rotting animals and plants with a microscope.
- Scientists thought these organisms were being produced by the rotting matter.
- They believed these organisms were getting into people's bodies and making them ill.

Pasteur's Germ Theory

In the late 1850s, French scientist **Louis Pasteur** was trying to discover why alcohol and milk turned sour. He published his findings, which he called **Germ Theory**, in 1861:

 → →

| **1** Microbes, which Pasteur called germs, made liquids turn sour. | **2** Germs were in the air – when liquids were sealed, they did not turn sour. | **3** Germs were destroyed by sterilisation (heating the liquid). |

By 1865, he proved that germs caused disease, which he explained in detail in his 1878 publication *Germ Theory and its Application to Medicine*.

People were initially quick to criticise Germ Theory because they thought that it was unlikely that deadly diseases were caused by minuscule microbes. However, Pasteur's theory eventually gained acceptance, and his work influenced other scientists and doctors including Robert Koch (**page 20**) and Joseph Lister (**page 24**).

Koch's work on microbes

German doctor Robert Koch used Pasteur's ideas to identify the microbe that caused anthrax in 1875. His findings were published in 1876. He and his team of scientists went on to:

- Identify the microbes causing tuberculosis (known as TB) (in 1882) and cholera (in 1883).
- Discover that chemical dyes stained some microbes, which made them easier to see under a microscope.
- Develop a steam steriliser to kill microbes (see **page 50**).

Factors for change

Improving and new technology

Better microscopes and stains helped scientists see 'animalcules' (**page 11**) more clearly.

Key individuals

The work of Dr John Snow (see **page 28**) and Joseph Lister (see **page 24**) helped convince people Pasteur and Koch's work was correct.

Faster transport and communication

Steam trains meant books and people (and therefore ideas) could reach others much faster than before.

Factors for resistance to change

Beliefs and attitudes

People still believed in old ideas and were slow to accept new ones.

Other scientists

There was fierce debate throughout the 1870s between scientists who supported Germ Theory, such as John Tyndall, and those who supported Spontaneous Generation, such as Henry Bastian.

Government

The British government refused to accept Germ Theory initially. Instead, they believed in the miasma theory.

The influence of Pasteur and Koch

It took time for Germ Theory to become known in Britain and even longer for people to believe it, but eventually Pasteur and Koch's work would have huge influence on medicine:

- It would lead to successful ways to treat and prevent disease.
- Both scientists inspired others and helped attract funding from governments, individuals and businesses, leading to more medical research and more discoveries.
- By 1900, germs were accepted as the cause of disease by most people in Britain. More people were able to prevent illness by trying to keep themselves and their homes clean.

Explain why there was progress in explaining the cause of disease in the period c1700–c1900.

You **may** use the following in your answer:

- Spontaneous Generation
- Germ Theory

You **must** also use information of your own. [12]

Your answer may include:

Spontaneous Generation:

- *Spontaneous Generation was the theory that microbes were produced from rotting matter, and these microbes were responsible for making people ill. This contributed to progress in medicine because people began to believe that microbes could make someone ill.*

Germ Theory:

- *Pasteur developed Germ Theory in 1861 when he noticed that unsealed liquids turned sour which suggested that germs were in the air rather than produced by rotting matter. He proved that microbes were the cause of disease. Pasteur's work helped to explain the causes of disease and influenced other scientists.*

Other information:

- *Robert Koch built on the work of Pasteur, and he identified the microbes which caused anthrax, TB and cholera in the 1870–80s.*
- *Koch discovered that chemical dyes could be used to make microbes more visible under a microscope which made identifying microbes easier.*
- *The work of Koch and Pasteur inspired other scientists, such as Joseph Lister, and attracted funding from governments and businesses which helped lead to more research and discoveries into the causes of disease.*
- *Increasing beliefs in science meant that by 1900 very few people believed in religious or supernatural causes of disease, most people accepted that germs contributed to illness and that keeping yourself and your home clean could be an effective way to keep germs at bay.*
- *Improvements in microscopes allowed scientists to see microbes more clearly.*
- *The introduction of steam trains meant that ideas could travel much faster than ever before so this contributed to progress in understanding disease.*

This question should be marked in accordance with the levels-based mark scheme on page 66.

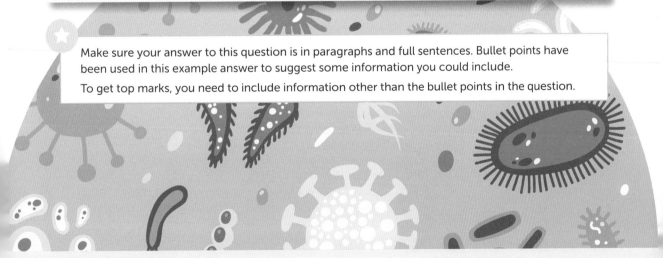

Make sure your answer to this question is in paragraphs and full sentences. Bullet points have been used in this example answer to suggest some information you could include.

To get top marks, you need to include information other than the bullet points in the question.

THE EXTENT OF CHANGE IN CARE AND TREATMENT, c1700–c1900

By 1900, treatment and ways of preventing disease had changed dramatically from 1700. However, some similarities remained.

Hospitals in the 18th century

During the 18th century, new hospitals began appearing across the country. They were mostly funded by rich donors and doctors willing to do some charity work.

As more and more people attended hospitals, the conditions got worse and worse. Hospitals had separate wards for infectious patients, but doctors lacked the knowledge to wash or change between patients and diseases spread quickly. It took an inspiring woman to bring change (see below).

Factors for change

Attitudes towards hospitals had changed. Hospitals were now places of medicine, not religion. Doctors visited regularly and there was an onsite surgeon or apothecary as well as women acting as untrained nurses and helpers.

Some poor people who could not afford medical bills finally had access to trained doctors.

Florence Nightingale

Florence Nightingale (1820–1910) had a religious conviction to help people and decided to become a nurse in the 1840s, aged around 20. She became a superintendent of nurses at King's College Hospital in London in 1854.

Following newspaper reports of poor conditions in British hospitals during the **Crimean War** (1853–56), Nightingale convinced the government to send her and a team of nurses out there.

Impact of Florence Nightingale

- Her team improved the cleanliness of the hospitals and patients in Crimea and provided valued nursing care.

- The death rate reduced from 40% to 2%, although this was largely due to the Sanitary Commission repairing the sewers that were leaking into the water supply. Nightingale returned to England a national hero.

- In 1859, she wrote *Notes on Nursing* and in 1860, she established the Nightingale School for Nurses which taught the importance of cleanliness and hygiene.

- In 1863 she wrote *Notes on Hospitals* which influenced how hospitals were run and built.

Impact on hospitals

- 'Pavilion' style hospitals were created with separate wards to keep the infectious apart, with larger rooms and more windows to improve ventilation.
- New hospitals were made from materials that were easier to clean. They had clean water supplies, good sewers and plenty of washing facilities for people and equipment.
- Nightingale's training turned nursing into a respectable, skilled occupation. Numbers of nurses rose, and they improved medical care.

Surgery in the 18th century

Surgery in the 18th century was dangerous. The three big problems were:

Bleeding

Patients could die from blood loss.

Pain

Patients could die from shock.

Infection

Patients could contract a fatal infection during surgery.

Bleeding remained a problem throughout the 19th century despite surgeons operating as quickly as possible to increase their patients' chances of survival.

The impact of anaesthetics on surgery

Pain during surgery was a problem because:

- patients could die from shock.
- patients could not always lie still, so surgeons made mistakes.
- only simple, quick surgery could be attempted.
- patients were reluctant to have surgery.

Humphry Davy, **1795**: discovered **laughing gas** (nitrous oxide) which was used to numb pain for simple operations.

Clarke (**1842**) and **Liston** (**1846**): experimented with **ether** as an **anaesthetic**, but it caused unpleasant side-effects and was highly flammable.

James Simpson, **1847**: discovered the use of **chloroform** as an effective anaesthetic. However, if the dose was too high it could affect the heart and cause fatalities.

James Simpson and friends discover chloroform's effects.

Queen Victoria used chloroform to relieve the pain during childbirth in 1853, which increased the popularity of chloroform.

! Note

Developing effective pain relief helped longer and more complex operations to take place. However, this also increased the problem of infection, so the death rate actually increased.

The impact of antiseptics on surgery

Up until the mid-1800s, surgery was unhygienic. Surgeons would wear old, blood-soaked aprons to protect their clothes and surgical instruments weren't cleaned between patients. This massively increased the risk of patients contracting an infection during an operation.

Building on the work of Pasteur, **Joseph Lister** introduced **carbolic acid** to tackle infection in 1865. He realised that soaking bandages and spraying the air with carbolic acid during operations helped to prevent infection. This was one of the first attempts at **antiseptic** surgery (killing germs near surgical wounds). Lister published his results in a medical journal, *The Lancet*.

Take-up of carbolic acid in surgery was slow because:
* Many people still didn't accept Germ Theory.
* Carbolic acid made skin sore, and it smelt unpleasant.
* Lister encouraged colleagues to try it rather than scientifically proving the theory behind it.

Lister stopped using carbolic acid in 1890, but it slowly helped to change attitudes towards antiseptic surgery. Surgeons eventually began moving towards **aseptic** surgery (**page 50**), where germs were prevented from entering surgical wounds. By 1900, wearing protective surgical outfits and sterilising surgical equipment were the norm.

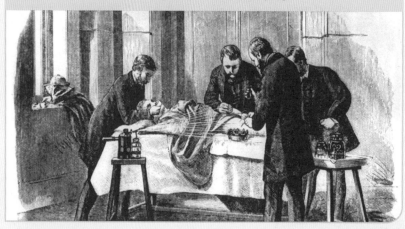

An operation performed under antiseptic conditions, including Lister's carbolic spray.

Explain **one** way in which ideas about surgery were different in 1900 from ideas in 1700. [4]

In 1700, speed was the key ingredient to good surgery to minimise pain and blood loss.[1] Doctors were unaware of germs and the dangers of infection and so did not try to keep themselves, or the surgical environment, clean.[1]

By 1900, thanks to Lister's work with carbolic acid and Pasteur's Germ Theory, the need for aseptic surgery to prevent infection was accepted.[1] Cleaning surgical equipment, operating theatres and clothing were adopted.[1]

This is just one example of a difference in surgery in the years 1900 and 1700. There are several other valid points that you could make.

CASE STUDY
JENNER AND THE DEVELOPMENT OF VACCINATION

Smallpox was one of the deadliest diseases of the 18th century. In 1796 Edward Jenner discovered how to prevent it, saving the lives of millions.

The work of Jenner

Dr Edward Jenner wanted to test the idea that people who had caught the much milder **cowpox** did not catch **smallpox**:

1. Jenner injected pus from cowpox blisters into 8-year-old James Phipps. Phipps became mildly ill with cowpox.
2. A few weeks later, Jenner infected Phipps with smallpox. Phipps did not become ill.
3. A few months later, Jenner infected Phipps with smallpox again. He did not become ill.

Jenner repeated the experiment many times. He called the process **vaccination** (after '*vacca*', Latin for cow). From 1798, Jenner published and promoted his findings, but it took a long time for vaccination to become widespread in Britain.

Smallpox and inoculation

Before Jenner, smallpox was prevented by **inoculation** where pus from smallpox was put into a cut of a healthy person. This usually meant the patient got a mild case of smallpox, but it prevented death because once the patient recovered, they didn't catch it again. However, some patients contracted a fatal case of smallpox from inoculation. Inoculators charged a lot of money for their services, so few could afford it.

Reasons why uptake of vaccination was slow

- Many scientists, including members of the Royal Society, did not initially support it.
- No one could explain why it worked.
- People didn't like the idea of being given an animal disease.
- Many doctors did not promote it – they were making money from inoculation.
- Sometimes it looked like it didn't work because people did not do it correctly.

Government intervention made the difference

- 1840 — the government paid for children's smallpox vaccinations.
- 1853 — smallpox vaccination became compulsory.
- 1871 — compulsory smallpox vaccination was enforced.
- 1900 — the smallpox death rate reduced from over 1,000 people per million in 1800 to almost 0.

Jenner's vaccination did not directly lead to more vaccinations because it relied on a unique link between cowpox and smallpox. It would be over 80 years before the next vaccination was developed (see page 26).

NEW APPROACHES TO PREVENTION, c1700–c1900

The development and use of vaccinations

Louis Pasteur, inspired by Jenner (see **page 25**) wanted to find more ways of preventing disease.

In 1879, chicken cholera was having a huge impact on French farming. Pasteur used Koch's methods to find the microbe that caused the disease. He instructed his team to inject the microbe into some chickens. One of Pasteur's team ran out of time before the laboratory shut down for the summer break. When he returned several weeks later, he injected his batch of chickens with the microbe anyway. The chickens injected with the microbe that had been exposed to oxygen did not die from the injection, unlike other chickens, and they did not become seriously ill from chicken cholera. Leaving the microbe had made it weaker, and injecting the weakened version gave the chickens a milder form of the disease but protected them from getting the disease severely in the future. Pasteur suggested that vaccines could be found for all diseases.

Further vaccines

Pasteur's team then developed vaccines for anthrax and rabies. In 1885, he tested his vaccine for rabies on humans. Other scientists then began work on developing vaccines for more diseases.

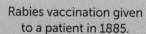

Rabies vaccination given to a patient in 1885.

Factors for change

- Previous discoveries by Jenner, Pasteur and Koch.
- Improving technology, e.g. **syringes** were invented in 1853.
- Funding from governments and private individuals for continuing medical research.

Explain **one** way in which ideas about preventing disease were different in 1900 from ideas in 1500. [4]

In 1500, many people believed that disease was caused by God so ideas about preventing disease were often based in religion.[1] For example, people would pray, fast or whip themselves to try to prevent disease.[1]

By 1900, thanks to Pasteur's Germ Theory, most people accepted that disease was caused by germs, so ways to prevent disease were more scientific.[1] For example, Jenner's work on developing a smallpox vaccination led to government-funded vaccination campaigns to prevent the spread of smallpox.[1]

This is just one example of a difference in disease prevention in 1900 and 1500. There are several other valid points that you could make.

The Public Health Act (1875)

In 1700, the government had very little involvement in public health, but by 1875 things had changed and the government passed a **Public Health Act** making it compulsory for towns and cities to provide **public health provisions**.

"Monster soup commonly called Thames water" (1828). People knew that dirty water contributed to illness.

Factors for change

- 19th century **epidemics** of deadly diseases such as **cholera** (see **page 28**).

- A report in 1842 by Edwin Chadwick suggested that poor living conditions contributed to poor health and lower life expectancy, especially in urban areas. The average life expectancy of a labourer in Manchester was 17 years old.

- **The Great Stink** (1858) — hot weather in the summer of 1858 caused filth in the River Thames to cause an awful smell in London, which led to calls to clean up the river and the introduction of a sewer network.

- A growing belief in **Germ Theory** due to the work of people like John Snow (see **page 19**).

- Changes to voting laws (1867) meant politicians needed the votes of working-class men who lived in more deprived areas.

- The **technology** of the industrial revolution, e.g. pumps and pipes.

The Public Health Act, 1875

- Every local authority had to employ medical officers to monitor the health of people in that area.
- Every local authority had to employ sanitary inspectors to regularly check public health facilities.
- Local authorities were allowed to raise taxes to pay for public health provision.

By 1900, all towns and cities had:

- Clean water supplies
- Drains and sewers
- Public toilets
- Street lighting
- Regular rubbish collections and street cleaning.

Impact of the Public Health Act

The Public Health Act led to a reduction in the number of outbreaks of infectious diseases caused by poor sanitation, for example, the last cholera epidemic in Britain was in 1866. Following the Act, there was a reduction in the death rate, and life expectancy slowly improved. The Act also set a precedent for the government taking more responsibility for public health.

CASE STUDY
FIGHTING CHOLERA IN LONDON (1854)

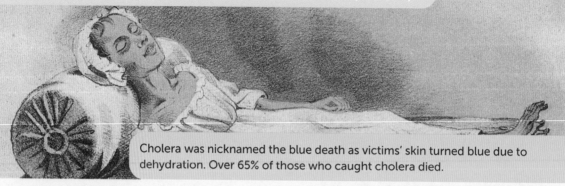

Cholera was nicknamed the blue death as victims' skin turned blue due to dehydration. Over 65% of those who caught cholera died.

The first **cholera** epidemic hit Britain in 1831–32, killing 20,000 people. It spread rapidly, causing diarrhoea and vomiting and could kill within hours.

Attempts to prevent its spread

Prior to Germ Theory, people thought cholera was caused by miasma, so they burnt bonfires and barrels of tar or smoked tobacco to drive away impure air. Praying and keeping homes clean were also used to prevent the spread of cholera.

John Snow and the Broad Street pump

Dr John Snow lived and worked in Soho, London. During another cholera outbreak in 1848 he believed that cholera was caused by something that was ingested (eaten or drunk). Few believed him. In 1854 when cholera arrived in Soho again, Snow tried to prove his theory.

1. He marked where cholera victims lived on a map of Soho (right).
2. This helped him to see that one water pump – the **Broad Street pump** – was at the centre of these people's homes.
3. He interviewed residents to find out where they got their water.
4. He found those who had used the Broad Street pump had contracted cholera, whereas those who used another water source had not.
5. He took the handle off the pump, so people had to get water from elsewhere.
6. The number of deaths quickly fell.

It was later discovered that the Broad Street outbreak had been caused by the water supply being contaminated by a nearby cesspool (underground container for the storage of waste).

Snow reported his findings to a government committee, but they thought the deaths were caused by miasma around the water pump rather than the water itself, so took no action.

'Government action in the years c1700–c1900 had the biggest impact on preventing disease.'

How far do you agree? Explain your answer.

You **may** use the following in your answer:

- the Public Health Act, 1875
- the work of Edward Jenner

You **must** also use information of your own.   [16 for content + 4 for SPaG = 20]

Your answer may include:

Agree:

- *Jenner's work on vaccinations provided a way to prevent smallpox. However, his work was not accepted by scientists because no one could explain why it worked, and it was rejected by the public because people didn't like the idea of being infected with a disease from cows.*
- *Government support and vaccination campaigns, for example making smallpox vaccination compulsory from 1853, helped to promote Jenner's work and dramatically reduce the impact of smallpox. Within 100 years, the death rate decreased from 1,000 per million to almost 0.*
- *By 1875, following multiple outbreaks of cholera and the Great Stink, the government recognised that they had a responsibility for looking after people's health.*
- *In 1875, the Public Health Act introduced medical officers to monitor the health of local people, and sanitary inspectors to check public health facilities. By 1900, all towns and cities had access to clean water, drains and sewers, as well as regular rubbish collections and street cleaning. These changes helped to improve public health, increase life expectancy and prevent the spread of disease.*

Disagree:

- *The government couldn't have introduced the smallpox vaccination without the work of Jenner, so his individual contribution had more of an impact.*
- *In 1854, John Snow noticed that an outbreak of cholera was centred around a water pump in Broad Street. Snow removed the pump handle and ended the outbreak.*
- *Snow reported his findings to a government committee to try to prevent further deaths, but they thought that the outbreak was caused by miasma, rather than the water, so they didn't take any immediate action. This meant that the government hindered disease prevention.*
- *New technology, such as pumps and pipes, meant that the government was able to provide fresh water and sewage systems introduced by the Public Health Act. Without these inventions, the impact of the government's Public Health Act would not have been as significant.*

This question should be marked in accordance with the levels-based mark scheme on page 67.

To get top marks, you must refer back to the question and make a judgement on the statement, having outlined the different sides of the argument. You also need to include information other than the bullet points in the question.

Make sure your answer to this question is in paragraphs and full sentences. Bullet points have been used in this example answer to suggest some information you could include.

ADVANCES IN UNDERSTANDING THE CAUSES OF ILLNESS AND DISEASE, c1900–PRESENT

During c1900–present, scientists have discovered the causes of more diseases.

Viruses

In 1898, a Dutch scientist called Martinus Beijernick discovered that some microbes were different to bacteria. He called them viruses.

While bacterial infections can be cured with antibiotics, such as penicillin (see **page 37**), viruses can only be killed by the body's immune system. This means, despite advances in modern medicine, viruses can be difficult to treat. Influenza (the flu) is an example of a virus. Although vaccinations can help prevent the flu, it still causes tens of thousands of deaths each year.

Genetic factors

By the 1930s, scientists proved what had long been suspected – some diseases are **inherited** (passed on from parents to their children). Examples of genetic diseases include cystic fibrosis and sickle-cell anaemia.

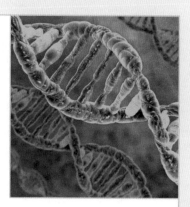

By the 1950s, x-ray crystallography meant scientists could see **DNA** (right) – a substance in cells containing **genetic** instructions. In 1953, **James Watson** and **Frances Crick** mapped the structure of DNA. Watson then led the **Human Genome Project** (1990–2000) to map the DNA in every cell in the human body. Since 2000, research is ongoing to:

- find how the DNA of genetic conditions is different, to learn more about them.
- research possible treatments for genetic conditions and diseases.
- discover which genes are linked to certain diseases, for example, types of cancer.

Scientists now have a better understanding of inherited diseases and can help to treat genetic conditions using **gene therapy**, which helps to repair or reconstruct defective genes.

Factors for change

Scientists could see **genetic material** due to more powerful electron microscopes, invented in 1931.

Lifestyle factors

Throughout the 20th century, doctors have used science and technology to monitor people's health to understand the lifestyle factors that impact wellbeing. We now know that smoking can cause various illnesses, including lung cancer (see **page 40**), too much alcohol can cause liver damage, too much sunlight can cause skin cancer and being overweight can lead to diabetes.

IMPROVEMENTS IN DIAGNOSIS, c1900–PRESENT

Diagnosing illness

In 1900, doctors diagnosed illness much as they had in 1700 – through observing their patients' symptoms and using their own knowledge that had been passed on by other doctors. Doctors continue to do this in the 21st century but they now use a huge variety of tests to help them.

Seeing inside the body

Doctors can now see inside the body to help them diagnose problems without performing surgery. Since the invention of **x-ray** machines in 1895, different **scans** have been used, such as ultrasound and MRI scans. Tiny cameras can also be inserted into the body, for example using **endoscopes** or **keyhole surgery**. These techniques help to diagnose patients earlier, and with greater accuracy.

Laboratory testing

Doctors also use scientific testing, either themselves or in a laboratory, to examine blood, urine and body tissue for a huge range of conditions. **Blood tests** can be used to check a person's cholesterol level, which can indicate someone's likelihood of having a stroke. Blood tests can also be used to diagnose genetic conditions, or whether a person has cancer. Blood tests allow doctors to be more accurate in their diagnosis of conditions.

Monitors

Since the 1880s, monitors have been used to measure blood pressure. These monitors are useful because high blood pressure can cause damage to the heart. From the 1900s, machines have been used to check things such as blood sugar levels and heart rate. Some monitors can be used by patients at home. This has given people with health issues more control over their condition.

Factors for change

Science and technology have had a huge impact on improving diagnosis since 1900.

The **NHS** (see **page 33**) has also improved diagnosis. People now have checks and are screened for diseases even when they are not displaying any symptoms which helps early diagnosis.

THE EXTENT OF CHANGE IN CARE AND TREATMENT, c1900–PRESENT

Understanding that microbes cause disease led to the development of medicines in the 20th century that would kill microbes.

Magic bullets

From 1896, **Paul Ehrlich** who had worked with Robert Koch (see **page 20**) was given German government funding for his own research team. He believed he could find a chemical compound that would kill a specific microbe. In 1905, Ehrlich focused his research on syphilis and the chemical **Salvarsan**. In 1909, Sahachiro Hata joined the team. He reviewed the work and found that the 606th compound that had been rejected, actually worked.

Ehrlich used the term **magic bullets** as he looked for a chemical compound that would only 'shoot' a specific microbe and not damage the patient.

This was the first example of **chemotherapy** which is a chemical treatment for disease. It had many side-effects so was not used much. The second magic bullet **Prontosil**, (right) developed by Gerhard Domagk in 1932 as a cure for some infections, was more successful. It led to the discovery of chemicals that treated diseases including pneumonia, gonorrhoea and scarlet fever in the 1940s.

Factors for change

Advances in medicines were made due to key individuals and their teams, as well as funding by governments, private companies and charities. There was also a good amount of luck involved.

Antibiotics

Antibiotics kill bacteria just like synthetically formed chemical compounds but by using other bacteria. The first to be discovered was **penicillin** (see **page 37**) which led to the discovery of more antibiotics for different diseases. The impact of antibiotics on medical treatment was enormous. People that would previously have died could now be cured.

Researching and producing drugs has become very lucrative. Pharmaceutical companies are constantly finding and improving synthetic treatments for disease.

! Note

Superbugs have developed a resistance to antibiotics which means antibiotics are becoming less effective.

Explain **one** way in which medical treatment in the years c1250–c1500 was different from medical treatment in the years c1900–present. [4]

In the years c1250–c1500, people used treatments to balance the humours based on the ideas of Hippocrates.[1] He believed that purging and bleeding would remove the excess humour that was causing disease.[1] In the years c1900–present, people use antibiotics or synthetic drugs created by scientists.[1] These cure people by killing the microbe causing the disease.[1]

The impact of the NHS

Prior to 1948, only school-aged children were eligible for free check-ups (from 1907) and treatment (from 1912), and workers' medical care was paid for by the **1911 National Insurance Act**. This meant many people, especially housewives, very young children and the elderly, who suffered from poor health couldn't afford access to medical care.

The NHS was introduced in 1948 and gave everyone access to free healthcare. People could now:

Call an ambulance and get emergency care

Visit a GP when they were unwell

Receive hospital care

Get hospital treatment, including surgery

Receive maternity care before, during and after birth

Get medicines prescribed by a doctor

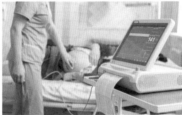

The NHS is funded through taxes. However, the huge costs of running the NHS led to some charges being introduced, e.g. in 1951, people in work had to pay for prescriptions.

Gradually, the NHS improved the health provision and treatment that was available in Britain:

- Hospitals became nationally run. In the following decades, more hospitals were built in different parts of the country, including specialist hospitals. The Quality Care Commission helped raise and equalise hospital standards.
- It helped train more medical professionals. The number of doctors doubled between 1948–1973.
- It helps fund research into new treatments.

Factors for change

Changing attitudes meant that more people believed that the government had a responsibility for providing healthcare for everyone.

Impact of science and technology — high-tech medicine and surgery

Hospital treatment has evolved since 1900. This is due to surgeons' increased knowledge and skill, better technology, and funding. More conditions can be treated than ever before.

- **Blood transfusions** (see **page 51**) have been used, especially since the 1940s, to replace blood lost during and after surgery.

- **Radiotherapy** (since the early 1900s) and cancer **chemotherapy** (since the 1940s) are used to treat some cancers.

- Since 1945, **dialysis machines** have helped people with kidney disease.

- **Plastic surgery** has developed since the First World War (see **page 52**).

- From the 1930s, **anaesthetics** have developed so they are injected, rather than inhaled meaning that dosage is more controlled.

- **Joint and bone replacement operations** have increased thanks to surgical skill plus the design and development of artificial joints.

- **Heart bypass operations** were common by the 1970s thanks to machines that maintain circulation and microsurgery (using very small instruments).

- **Pacemakers** have been used to treat abnormal heart rhythms since the 1950s.

- **Organ transplants** have been carried out since the 1950s and **bone marrow transplants** since 1986. **Tissue typing**, where the donor and patient's tissues are analysed, helps prevent the recipient's body from rejecting the donor.

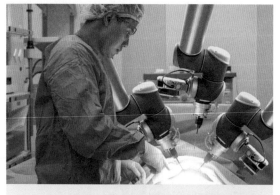

Robots have been carrying out surgery since the 1980s. They are particularly useful for very precise work on a micro scale.

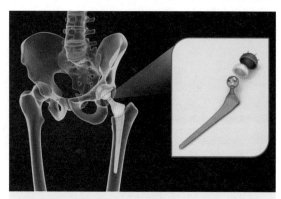

The first total hip replacement was done in 1962. They are very common today.

A patient on a kidney dialysis machine.

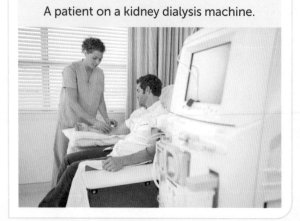

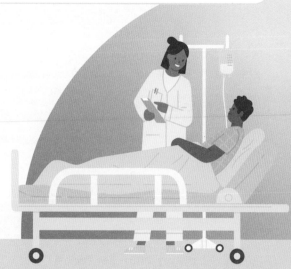

NEW APPROACHES TO PREVENTION, c1900–PRESENT

Since 1900, the national government has intervened in public health to improve living conditions and prevent illness.

Mass vaccinations

By 1920, many vaccinations had been developed but few people could afford them, except for those (such as smallpox see **page 25**) which were organised and paid for by local health boards.

The first nationally funded vaccination campaign was for **diphtheria** in 1940. By 1957, the number of diphtheria deaths had decreased from 3,000 in 1940 to just 6.

Since then, **mass vaccination** has helped prevent many diseases. A successful polio vaccine was introduced in 1956 and the disease was almost eradicated in Britain by the 1970s.

Government lifestyle campaigns

As more is known about how lifestyle factors can impact disease (see **page 30**), the government and the NHS have run **lifestyle campaigns** to try to educate people to make healthier choices. Campaigns use posters, information leaflets and TV advertisements. They have focused on:

- raising awareness of a disease and how to prevent it, e.g. AIDS: don't die of ignorance
- the dangers of certain activities, e.g. smoking
- the positive impact of certain activities, e.g. eating 5 a day

Charities also fund lifestyle campaigns. For example, Alcohol Concern runs a Dry January campaign to encourage people to give up drinking alcohol for a month.

Public health laws

In 1952, air pollution in London led to the **Great Smog**. It caused upwards of 4,000 deaths, as well as showing that air pollution could contribute to breathing difficulties, such asthma and bronchitis. The government introduced the Clean Air Act, 1956 to try to control air pollution and improve air quality in towns and cities.

The NHS provides health checks and screening to spot signs that may cause illness and helps people to lose weight or give up smoking.

Explain why there has been progress in diagnosing illness since c1900.

You **may** use the following in your answer:

- blood tests
- the NHS

You **must** also use information of your own.   [12]

Your answer may include:

Blood tests:

- *Doctors can use laboratory testing to diagnose a patient earlier and with greater accuracy. Blood tests can diagnose a huge range of conditions, for example, whether a person has cancer or a genetic disease.*

The NHS:

- *The NHS made healthcare freely available to everyone in the UK. It gave patients access to highly trained GPs, who can diagnose patients or refer them to specialists for further tests.*
- *The NHS also runs screening checks which means that people can be checked for diseases before they even display any symptoms. This helps to diagnose patients early.*

Other information:

- *Other laboratory tests can be used to check a person's urine or tissue to diagnose conditions.*
- *The discovery of DNA in the 1930s proved that some diseases are genetic, such as cystic fibrosis. This helped to diagnose inherited conditions. The discovery of DNA led to the Human Genome project which mapped DNA to learn more about how genes are linked to illnesses.*
- *In 1898, Beijernick discovered viruses. This allowed doctors to diagnose viral infections.*
- *Advancements in technology, such as the introduction of the x-ray machine in 1895, meant doctors could look inside a patient's body and diagnose illnesses without performing surgery. Other non-invasive scans, such as MRI and ultrasound scans, also help to diagnose patients.*
- *Doctors can also use monitors to check a person's blood pressure, as well as blood sugar levels and heart rate which can help to diagnose medical conditions.*

This question should be marked in accordance with the levels-based mark scheme on page 66.

Make sure your answer to this question is in paragraphs and full sentences. Bullet points have been used in this example answer to suggest some information you could include.

To get top marks, you need to include information other than the bullet points in the question.

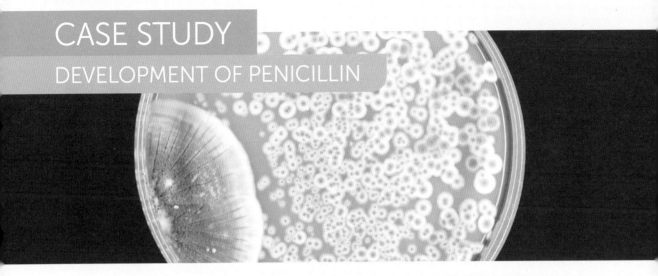

CASE STUDY
DEVELOPMENT OF PENICILLIN

It took luck, the Second World War and the work of three men to discover and manufacture penicillin – the first **antibiotic**.

The work of Alexander Fleming (1881–1955)

In 1928, **Alexander Fleming** (right) a Scottish doctor, returned to his laboratory after a holiday to discover that mould had grown on a petri dish he had left out. This mould had killed some bacteria in the dish.

Fleming grew more of the mould and experimented to see which bacteria it could kill.

In 1929 he published his findings. The mould that he called **penicillin** killed many types of bacteria without harming the cells the bacteria lived in.

Fleming thought that penicillin could have a medicinal use, but he needed to find a chemist who could purify penicillin so it would work inside the human body.

Few seemed interested, and he could not get funding to continue his work, so he turned his attention to other projects.

The work of Howard Florey and Ernst Chain

1938

Florey read Fleming's findings on penicillin as his team researched ways to kill bacteria. He wanted to continue Fleming's work. Florey obtained funding from US drug companies after the British government refused to fund further research. **Chain**, part of Florey's team, developed a way to purify penicillin. Growing purified penicillin took time and lots of space, for example, gallons of liquid were needed to make an amount of penicillin the size of a fingernail.

1940

Eight mice were injected with a bacterial infection. Four mice were given a dose of penicillin, the other four mice were not. The mice that had been given penicillin survived, while the other mice died. The team began growing penicillin wherever they could.

1941

Penicillin was first tested on a human. It worked but the penicillin ran out before the man was totally cured so he died. Money was needed to produce penicillin on a massive scale. Florey again failed to get funding from the British government.

December 1941 — after joining the Second World War, the US government funded American drug companies to mass produce it.

1943

The British government finally funded British drug companies to mass produce penicillin in Britain. By the end of the war, penicillin had saved thousands of lives.

1946

The British public were able to buy penicillin if prescribed by a doctor.

Howard Florey

Ernst Chain

Fleming, along with Florey and Chain, received the Nobel Prize for medicine for their work on penicillin in 1945.

'The development of penicillin had the greatest impact on improving medical treatment in the period since c1800.'

How far do you agree? Explain your answer.

You **may** use the following in your answer:

- magic bullets
- advancements in technology

You **must** also use information of your own.   [16 for content + 4 for SPaG = 20]

Your answer may include:

Agree:

- *The penicillin mould discovered by Fleming could kill many types of bacteria without harming the cells the bacteria lived in. This finally provided a cure for diseases caused by bacteria and helped to cure many people who would have previously died, including thousands of soldiers during World War II.*

- *Florey and Chain took Fleming's mould and purified it. They helped to get government funding to produce it on an industrial scale. The mass production of penicillin helped to pave the way for the development of the pharmaceutical industry which has led to greater research and funding for medical treatment.*

Disagree:

- *Magic bullets, such as Salvarsan and Prontosil, helped to treat diseases such as syphilis. The development of chemotherapy – chemical treatments for disease – paved the way for further research into synthetic chemicals that can cure disease, such as pneumonia, gonorrhoea and scarlet fever. Prescribing synthetic chemicals is now one of the most common and effective methods of treatment.*

- *Technology has had an impact on improving medical treatment since 1800. For example, dialysis machines treat people with kidney disease, artificial bones and joints have been developed to replace those worn by age or damaged by injury and pacemakers are used to treat abnormal heart rhythms.*

- *Improvements in surgical knowledge, techniques and technology has had an enormous impact on improving medical treatment since 1800. Far more complex operations such as organ transplants have successfully treated conditions that would not have been treatable previously.*

This question should be marked in accordance with the levels-based mark scheme on page 67.

To get top marks, you must refer back to the question and make a judgement on the statement, having outlined the different sides of the argument. You also need to include information other than the bullet points in the question.

Make sure your answer to this question is in paragraphs and full sentences. Bullet points have been used in this example answer to suggest some information you could include.

CASE STUDY

THE FIGHT AGAINST LUNG CANCER IN THE 21ST CENTURY

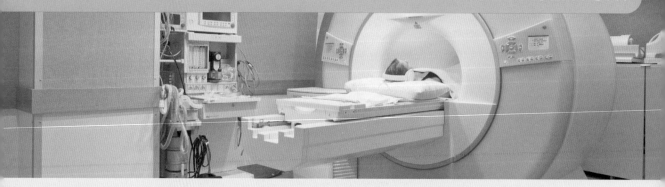

From 1900 until the 1990s, there was a significant increase in the number of people with lung cancer. Efforts have been made to treat and prevent it.

The use of science and technology in diagnosis and treatment

Doctors use a combination of science and technology to diagnose lung cancer in the 21st century. Patients usually have a CT scan, followed by a biopsy using a bronchoscope if the scan shows suspected cancer. The sample is analysed to diagnose what is wrong and to help the doctor work out how advanced the cancer is and how it should be treated.

A few patients with lung cancer undergo surgery to remove the tumour. Very few have lung transplants. Most patients have either radiotherapy or chemotherapy.

Death rates have fallen, but lung cancer survival rates are still very low. It is the third most common cancer in Britain but causes the greatest number of cancer deaths. Only 1 in 10 people diagnosed with lung cancer survive for 10 or more years.

Government action

Around 79% of lung cancer cases are preventable, with 72% caused by smoking. The government's prevention measures focused on reducing smoking. Many lifestyle campaigns give information on the damage smoking can cause. Laws have also been introduced:

- It is illegal to advertise any tobacco product and shops cannot display these products. They are kept behind shutters.
- Smoking has been banned in public places since 2007.
- Taxes on tobacco products are high so the cost of the product is high.
- From 2017, cigarette packets must show text and photos warning of the dangers of smoking.

Since 2000, instances of lung cancer have dropped but there are still nearly 50,000 cases a year.

EXAMINATION PRACTICE

1. Explain **one** way in which the methods used by doctors to diagnose illness during the medieval period (c1250–c1500) were different from those used during the renaissance (c1500–c1700). [4]

2. Explain why medical treatments in c1250–1500 were largely ineffective.

    You may use the following in your answer:
    - the theory of opposites
    - bloodletting

    You **must** also use information of your own. [12]

3. 'The Public Health Act of 1875 was the most significant factor in preventing illness during the period c1850–present.'

    How far do you agree? Explain your answer.

    You may use the following in your answer:
    - the work of Pasteur
    - government lifestyle campaigns

    You **must** also use information of your own. [16 for content + 4 for SPaG = 20]

4. 'There was little progress in medical treatment in Britain c1500–c1900.'

    How far do you agree? Explain your answer.

    You may use the following in your answer:
    - the work of William Harvey
    - the influence of Florence Nightingale

    You **must** also use information of your own. [16 for content + 4 for SPaG = 20]

THE CONTEXT OF THE WESTERN FRONT

The Western Front was the area of northern France and Flanders (a region in Belgium) where the First World War was fought in western Europe.

The theatre of war: the Ypres salient, the Somme, Arras and Cambrai

Several battles took place on the British sector of the Western Front, many on the **Ypres** (pronounced *ee-pruh*) **salient** (a piece of land surrounded by enemy territory on three sides).

1914

3 August
Germany declared war on France.

4 August
Germany began advancing towards France through Belgium. Britain declared war on Germany.

6–9 September | Battle of the Marne
British troops, plus much larger French forces, stopped the German advance but only drove German troops back to the River Aisne, still in France. Both sides began digging **trenches** to defend their positions.

12 October–11 November | First Battle of Ypres
Germany increased its territory around Ypres. Britain held the town itself and could still access the English Channel.

> The term **theatre of war** is used to refer to an area where important military events are occurring.

1915

April | Battle for Hill 60
Britain captured this hill near Ypres, after exploding **mines** placed in tunnels which had been dug into it.

22 April–25 May | Second Battle of Ypres
Germany gained ground around Ypres. Germans first used **chlorine gas** (see **page 47**) as a weapon.

1916

1 July–18 November | The Somme
British forces made small gains and French forces made bigger gains. Huge loss of life on all sides with 20,000 British killed on first day. British first used tanks.

1917

9 April–16 May | Battle of Arras
In December 1916, the British began connecting and expanding the tunnels, caves and quarries at Arras. They had running water, electricity and a hospital. The tunnels, caves and quarries were used to protect troops and then to attack German lines in April 1917. British forces made small gains at the cost of high casualties.

31 July–6 November | Third Battle of Ypres (also known as Passchendaele)
British forces made some gains but with high casualties. Mud and rain defined the battle and many drowned.

20 November–8 December | Battle of Cambrai
First large-scale use of tanks caused high German casualties. Germans pushed back so no gains were made.

1918

11 November
Germany signed the armistice ending the fighting. By the end of the war, Britain had suffered nearly 3.2 million casualties, including 2.1 million injured. Most were on the Western Front.

The trench system

By the end of 1914, basic trenches ran from the English Channel to Switzerland. This developed into a complex system as the war continued. Early trenches were quickly dug by hand. Later, they were reinforced with bricks, wood and steel, and were about 6 feet (1.8 m) deep. Trenches could be damaged by enemy fire and bad weather, so needed constant maintenance. Support and reserve trenches were usually in better condition than the frontline trenches.

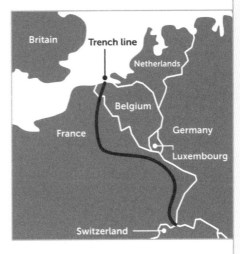

Pillbox
Soldiers firing machine guns were protected by concrete block houses.

Frontline trench
Attacks were launched from the frontline trench. Trenches were zigzagged so enemies could not fire a long way if they entered them.

Reserve trench
Troops were rested and counterattacks launched from the reserve trench.

Long-range artillery
Fired from behind the trenches at enemies advancing.

Rows of barbed wire slowed down enemy advances.

Dugouts in the support trench often contained basic furniture and stoves.

Support trench
The support trench (200–500 metres behind the frontline) was used for backup troops and retreat when trenches came under attack.

Communication trench
People and supplies were moved via communication trenches.

No Man's Land
The area between the two sets of trenches

Dugouts on the frontline trench provided some cover from attack.

The nature of the terrain and problems of transport and communication

The significance of the terrain for medical treatment

Getting wounded soldiers medical help quickly increased their chances of survival, but this was very difficult because:

- The narrow, often crowded and zig-zagged, trenches were difficult to move through.
- The ground around the trenches was usually very uneven with holes and craters caused by **shells** (explosives).
- There was little protection from the weather so the ground quickly became waterlogged and very muddy.
- The injured and those retrieving them were often still under attack.

A horse stuck in the mud of Flanders during a battle at Ypres.

The significance of transport and communication problems

Communications were often slow (carrier pigeons were still used) and telegraph and telephone lines were frequently destroyed which made it difficult to know where **stretcher-bearers** and ambulances needed to go.

All methods for transporting the wounded had disadvantages.

Stretcher bearers

Took at least two people, usually four, to carry one injured person.

- ⊕ The only option in no-man's land.
- ⊖ Too few men to transport all wounded.
- ⊖ Took a long time and very tiring.
- ⊖ High risk of dropping/further damaging the injured.

Horse-drawn ambulance

Two horses could transport four injured people but up to eight horses were needed in the muddiest conditions.

- ⊕ Less physically demanding than stretcher bearers.
- ⊖ Slower than motor vehicles.
- ⊖ Very bumpy which could make injuries worse.

Motor ambulance

- ⊕ The fastest, smoothest method close to the frontline.
- ⊖ None were provided at first and always too few for the number of wounded.
- ⊖ Unusable in deep mud.

Trains, barges and boats

- ⊕ Fast, relatively smooth and the injured could be treated while being transported – some even contained operating theatres.
- ⊖ Were not close to the frontline.

1. Describe **two** features of stretcher bearers on the Western Front. [4]

2. How could you follow up Source A to find out more about transporting the wounded on the Western Front? [4]

Source A: Wounded men on stretchers waiting for a horse-drawn ambulance.

1. *Feature 1*

   Stretcher bearers were used to transport wounded soldiers from the frontline fighting.[1] Each stretcher could hold one soldier and needed at least two stretcher bearers to carry the soldier.[1]

   Feature 2

   Stretcher bearers were the only option for getting soldiers from no-man's land.[1] This was often dangerous for both the wounded and the stretcher bearers as they might be caught by enemy gunfire and the terrain was often uneven which could cause the bearers to drop the wounded and cause more damage.[1]

2. ***Detail in Source A that I would follow up:*** *There are many wounded men waiting to be loaded into horse-drawn ambulances.[1]*

   Question I would ask: *Was there a lack of ambulances for transporting the wounded?[1]*

   What type of source I could use: *Personal records of ambulance drivers, such as diaries.[1]*

   How this might help answer my question: *It would help me to see whether drivers mention a shortage of ambulances.[1]*

CONDITIONS REQUIRING MEDICAL TREATMENT ON THE WESTERN FRONT

Most medical problems on the Western Front were caused by the trench environment, the nature of the fighting and the weapons used.

Ill health caused by the trench environment

Poor health was common. Trenches were very cold and damp, often muddy and waterlogged, and rats were everywhere. Two of the main health problems were **trench foot** and **trench fever**. Both caused serious problems for the army as so many soldiers were affected.

Trench foot

- Caused by getting feet wet for long periods which led to swollen feet, infection, and gangrene. Once **gangrene** had set in, the foot had to be amputated.
- Troops were given whale oil to put on their feet (to keep feet dry) and spare socks. Foot inspections became very common.
- Trenches became drier as pumps and drains were used to remove water and platforms were added to keep feet out of water.

Trench fever

- Symptoms included fever, headache, painful muscles and vomiting.
- Although it rarely led to death, few treatments were available, and it could last for months.
- It wasn't until 1918 that lice were found to cause trench fever. **Delousing stations** were used to get rid of lice regularly which reduced the number of soldiers who contracted the disease.

A medical officer inspecting the feet of the 12th Battalion, East Yorkshire regiment, 9 January 1918.

Dysentery

Soldiers had limited access to clean water and toilets which meant diseases such as **dysentery**, which caused diarrhoea, could easily spread.

Shell shock

Shell shock was a reaction to the stress of combat, which could cause men to panic, lose the ability to sleep, talk or behave rationally.

Describe **two** features of the trench environment that led to ill health. [4]

Feature 1
Trenches were often very wet and muddy as they had no cover from the rain and snow, and soldiers walking through the trenches increased the mud.[1] *Soldiers had to stand in the trenches for long periods which led to trench foot.*[1]

Feature 2
Trenches were cold and damp and attracted rats. They were also very crowded and there was little opportunity to wash or change clothes.[1] *As a result, lice thrived, and this led to high incidences of trench fever.*[1]

The nature and problems of wounds

Wounds from explosives

- Over half of wounds were from explosive **shells**, fired from **artillery** (weapons that could fire munitions further than guns).
- Explosives caused **blast injuries**, where parts of the body were blown away, and caused major blood loss.
- **Shrapnel** (fragments of a bomb) could penetrate deep into the body, damaging organs.

Wounds from guns

- Machine guns fired very quickly, leaving many bullets in the body.
- Rifles were slower but more accurate. Their bullets could penetrate very deep into the body.
- Bullets from both types of gun could fracture bones and damage organs.

Gas attacks

- Gas was a totally new weapon. Gas masks (right) were issued from 1915, but they were less effective if they had been damaged. They improved during the war.

- **Mustard gas** could suffocate and damage lungs as well as cause burns and blisters on the skin. **Phosgene** and **chlorine gas** could cause death by suffocation. **Tear gas** mostly caused short periods of blindness and coughing.

Head injuries

- In the trenches, soldiers' heads were the most likely parts of their bodies to get hit. An increased use of explosives made head injuries more common. (see **page 52**).

- By late 1915, the **Brodie helmet** (a steel helmet pictured above) was used to prevent deaths
- Brain injuries were difficult to diagnose, and medics had very little experience of brain surgery.
- Those who survived head injuries were often left with scars and parts of their faces missing.

Wound infection

- Preventing wounds from getting infected was difficult on the Western Front because much of the ground contained bacteria which got into the body either when the person was shot, hit with shrapnel or after laying on the ground. Infections from **tetanus** and **gas gangrene** (a form of gangrene infection that produces gas within tissue) could be fatal.
- Serum to protect against tetanus was given from late 1914 but nothing could prevent gas gangrene. Even soldiers with minor injuries had a high risk of dying from infection.

THE WORK OF THE RAMC AND FANY

Most medical care for British forces was provided by the **RAMC**. The wounded were treated in different areas known as the chain of **evacuation**.

The Royal Army Medical Corps (RAMC)

The RAMC was the section of the British Army responsible for healthcare and medical treatment.

- About 20,000 medical professionals from the RAMC went to serve with the armed forces in August 1914. Most were sent to the Western Front.
- Only 300 of these were nurses. They worked in **base hospitals** as it was thought women were unable to cope closer to the front line. Demand meant this soon changed – from 1915, nurses worked in casually **clearing stations** and **dressing stations** (see page 49).
- All who worked in the RAMC were given military ranks. None carried weapons.
- The **Field Ambulance** were mobile medical units. They set up and staffed regimental **aid posts** and **dressing stations**.
- By the end of the war in 1918, over 145,000 medical professionals worked for the RAMC, including over 10,000 nurses.

The First Aid Nursing Yeomanry (FANY)

FANY was made up of female volunteers. Most had no medical training or experience. Small numbers of FANY units arrived in France in 1914 but they worked for French or Belgium forces as the British army did not allow their help. This changed from 1 January 1916 when FANY was officially allowed to support the RAMC. They:

- drove motor ambulances.
- provided basic first aid during transportation and supported RAMC staff at base hospitals.
- delivered medical supplies and food.

Member of FANY with an ambulance, 1914.

THE STAGES OF TREATMENT AREAS AND TRANSPORT

There were stages of treatment areas for the wounded.

Wounded either walked or were carried by other soldiers or stretcher bearers.

1   Regimental aid post (RAP)

- Close to the front line in communication trenches, dugouts or even shell holes.
- Stretcher bearers helped medical officers (doctors) give first aid and pain relief.
- Some wounded were treated and sent back to fight, others were sent on to dressing stations.

Wounded either walked or were carried by stretcher bearers or, sometimes by horse-drawn or motor ambulance.

2   Dressing stations (ADS and MDS)

ADS – Advanced Dressing Stations and MDS – Main Dressing Stations

- Situated 400–1200 metres behind RAPs, in small buildings, dugouts or tents.
- Medical officers were assisted by orderlies, stretcher-bearers and, from 1915, nurses.
- Carried out basic treatments such as dressing wounds. The more seriously hurt were sent to casualty clearing stations.
- Patients could stay up to a week before being sent back to fight or moved on for further treatment.

Wounded taken by horse-drawn or motor ambulance.

3   Casualty clearing stations (CCS)

- Several miles behind the RAPs, in large buildings, often near railways.
- Large numbers of doctors, orderlies and some nurses.
- The wounded, thought to have no chance of survival, were given pain relief but not treated.
- The range of treatments increased as the war went on – it became more obvious that surgery and dealing with infection needed to happen as soon as possible.
- Once treated, men either stayed to recover before going back to fight or were sent on to a Base Hospital.

Wounded taken to base hospitals by motor ambulance, train or canal barges.

4   Base hospitals

- Large hospitals near the coast so the wounded could be sent back to Britain.
- Large numbers of staff from the RAMC, including specialists for different treatments.
- Plenty of beds so the wounded could stay for a while before going back to fight or sent back to Britain for discharge or further treatment.

THE HISTORICAL CONTEXT OF MEDICINE IN THE EARLY 20TH CENTURY

Several medical breakthroughs happened in the years before the First World War, which allowed medical advancements on the Western Front.

Understanding infection and aseptic surgery

The discovery of Germ Theory (see **page 19**) and the work of people such as Florence Nightingale (see **page 22**) and Joseph Lister (see **page 24**) led to improved methods to prevent infection. **Antiseptic** surgery, where germs were killed on or around wounds, laid the foundations for **aseptic** surgery, where germs were stopped from getting into the operating theatre at all.

By the 1890s:

- Medics wore rubber gloves, clean surgical gowns and caps, and regularly washed their hands. Patients wore clean gowns.

- All dressings and bandages were sterilised and regularly changed.

- **Neuber** and **von Bergmann** invented ways to sterilise the air of operating theatres over the heating system. Theatres were regularly, and thoroughly, washed with disinfectants.

- Robert Koch (see **page 20**) discovered that steam killed germs. His steam steriliser of 1878 was replaced with **autoclaves** (a sealed tank that could be heated to high temperatures) from 1881 to sterilise all surgical instruments.

Development of x-rays

X-rays, discovered by **Wilhelm Röntgen** in 1895 improved diagnosis. X-ray (radiology) departments opened in many hospitals from 1896. Early x-ray machines were large, heavy, fragile and slow, taking 90 minutes to x-ray a hand before needing to be left to cool down. This made their use limited. The health risks regarding harmful radiation levels were not yet understood.

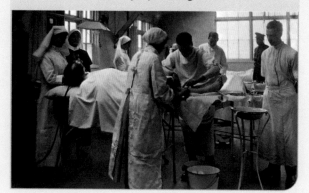

British army operating theatre.

Scientist Marie Curie built on Röntgen's work to develop the use of radiation in medical treatment. She also invented 'petit curies' small, mobile x-ray units which were used to diagnose the wounded in the First World War.

Blood transfusions and storage

Many injuries caused blood loss and all surgery involved some loss of blood. This was a major problem because it could lead to **shock**, where the organs shut down, causing death. There had been some progress in trying to restore lost blood:

James Blundell (physician)

Developed **blood transfusion** techniques between 1818–29. The patient and donor were directly connected because blood clots when it leaves the body, so it could not be stored. Transfusions were rarely attempted during the 19th century because sometimes they were successful and sometimes they failed and nobody knew why.

Almroth Wright

In 1894, he suggested certain acids could solve the issue of blood clotting and blocking transfusion tubes.

Karl Landsteiner

In 1901, he discovered blood types, including the universal Type O (a blood type that will be accepted by everybody). Until then, many patients received the wrong blood type and rejected the transfusion causing fever, kidney damage, and sometimes death.

Direct blood transfusion from 1876.

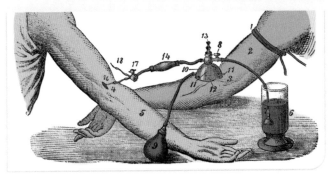

Blood transfusions were still rarely performed between 1901–15 because the right donor had to be found and had to sit with the patient while a transfusion was taking place. Blood could still not be stored.

Describe **two** features of medical breakthroughs by the start of the twentieth century. [4]

Feature 1
Joseph Lister's antiseptic surgery paved the way for aseptic surgery which was common by 1900. [1]
The operating theatre was regularly cleaned, instruments and bandages were sterilised and surgeons wore sterilised caps, gowns and rubber gloves which reduced the rate of infection during and after surgery. [1]

Feature 2
In 1895, Wilhelm Röntgen discovered x-rays and x-ray machines were developed. [1] *The machines were slow and bulky, but helped doctors diagnose problems such as broken bones.* [1]

SIGNIFICANCE OF THE WESTERN FRONT FOR SURGERY AND MEDICINE

Wounds on the Western Front led to developments in surgery and medicine.

New techniques in treating wounds and infection

Mobile x-ray units

From 1914, most base hospitals had an x-ray machine. Smaller, lighter units were developed which fitted inside vans so they could be moved to casualty clearing stations. The **mobile x-ray units** did not produce such clear images as static machines, but they helped diagnose broken bones and were vital in locating bullets and shrapnel.

Dealing with infection

Aseptic surgery in casualty clearing stations was impossible. However, bacteria were often already in the body.

Removing every tiny fragment of unwanted material from inside the body was essential. X-rays helped to locate unwanted material, and surgeons became more skilled at removing bullets and shrapnel but also soil and fabric.

Surgeons became experienced at removing infected and dead tissue which prevented infection from spreading.

Different antiseptics, such as carbolic lotion, did not always work. Two doctors developed the **Carrel-Dakin method** where a diluted acid was put into the wound through a tube. This was more successful and became common by 1917.

If all other methods failed, amputation was the only way to prevent death. Around a quarter of a million men lost limbs.

Head injuries

By 1918, those suffering from head wounds were far more likely to survive than in 1914 or 1915.

Medics improved at diagnosing brain injuries, and some became specialists. Patients were treated more quickly. Some casualty clearing stations only dealt with head injuries and there were specialised departments in base hospitals.

Surgeons discovered that operating on the head under local anaesthetic was far safer. Using a general anaesthetic could make the brain swell.

Harvey Cushing discovered that electromagnets could be used to remove even the smallest shrapnel fragments without causing further brain damage.

Harold Gillies developed ways to restore bone, skin and cartilage to rebuild faces. He set up a facial injuries clinic at Queen's Hospital in Sidcup which specialised in **plastic surgery**.

A soldier with a head injury shows the damage to his helmet.

Thomas splint

From 1916, the **Thomas splint** (right) was a device commonly strapped to a patient to keep broken legs still. It was quick and easy to fit and reduced pain. It prevented the joints from moving so it reduced the risk of further damage and major blood loss while the patient was transported. It significantly increased survival rates from broken legs, especially compound fractures (when bone breaks through the skin).

Dealing with blood loss

Blood transfusions were uncommon because medics distrusted them and used saline injections instead. A few person-to-person transfusions were performed in casualty clearing stations from 1915.

1

Several Canadian and American doctors improved the methods of person-to-person transfusion, using, for example, cannula and syringes. Although some of these included methods of one donor giving blood to more than one patient at a time, all required a donor to be present.

2

In 1915, American **Richard Lewisohn** found that adding sodium citrate stopped extracted blood from clotting, but the quality of blood quickly decreased so it could only be used for a few hours.

3

Fellow American **Richard Weil** found that storing citrated blood in cool temperatures stopped the blood deteriorating so it could be used for up to 2 days.

4

From 1915, Canadian, **Lawrence Bruce Robertson** experimented with different methods of delivering indirect blood transfusions using citrated blood. He helped prove the effectiveness of blood transfusions. From spring 1917, indirect transfusion was being done at CCSs, but blood often ran out.

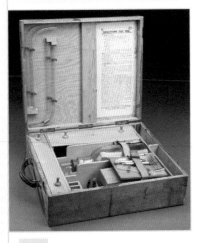

5

Later in 1917, **Geoffrey Keynes'** (British surgeon) blood transfusion kit (left) was carried by stretcher bearers and doctors in field ambulance units. It included equipment to transfer blood from another person as well as small quantities of blood in bottles which preserved life until the patient reached a CCS.

6

At the Battle of Cambrai (Nov–Dec 1917), American **Oswald Hope Robertson** stored O type blood mixed with sodium citrate and dextrose, in glass bottles surrounded by ice for 26 days. Only 20 patients were treated during battle but this was the first **blood bank** ever used.

KNOWLEDGE OF NATIONAL AND LOCAL SOURCES

Questions 2(a) and 2(b) will be source questions. You need to be aware of different national and local sources which might be used in enquiries (page 55).

Types of sources and what they may contain

Medical journals

Journals share articles between medical professionals to spread ideas and assess new techniques.

Military hospital records

Record details of soldiers and their injuries and treatments.

National newspapers

Contain news stories on battles and the number of casualties, latest developments or problems with medical treatments.

Local newspapers

Contain information on people from the local area and their experiences on the Western Front.

Photographs

These might show the wounded being transported or treated.

Personal accounts

E.g. letters and diaries that record the thoughts, actions and experiences of wounded soldiers, or those treating or transporting them such as stretcher bearers, ambulance drivers, doctors and nurses.

Army records

Contain military reports on events as well as information on individuals.

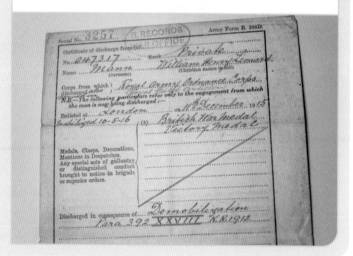

STRENGTHS AND WEAKNESSES OF DIFFERENT SOURCES FOR SPECIFIC ENQUIRIES

For both source questions in the exam, you need to know about the strengths and weaknesses of different sources for a specific enquiry.

What is an historical enquiry?

An enquiry is the specific topic that an historian is researching. Examples for this course might be:

1. Enquiry into the problems of carrying out medical treatment on the Western Front.

2. Enquiry into the work of ambulance drivers on the Western Front.

3. Enquiry into the effectiveness of new techniques in treating battle injuries on the Western Front.

The usefulness of sources

A source cannot be judged on its usefulness without knowing the enquiry. For example, an image of a horse-drawn ambulance would not be useful for enquiry 3. However, it would be of some use for enquiry 1 and it would be useful for enquiry 2.

How to assess usefulness

There are three aspects to consider when assessing the usefulness of a source. You need to consider all three of these to achieve good marks for question 2(a):

The source's content
Does the source contain anything related to the enquiry? How useful is this?

Your own knowledge
Does the source support or contradict what you already know?

The source's provenance
Do the **origins**, **nature** and **purpose** of the source make it more or less useful?

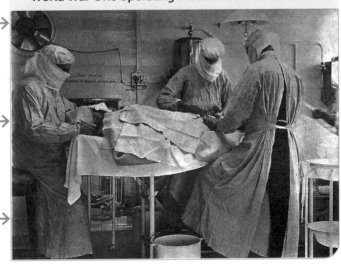
World War One operating theatre with three medics

Strengths and weakness of some different sources

Hospital records

➕ Usually give accurate information on medical treatments.

➕ Recorded by different people treating a patient, so not just one person's view.

➖ Sometimes records were not properly kept.

➖ Information is often brief and lacks detail.

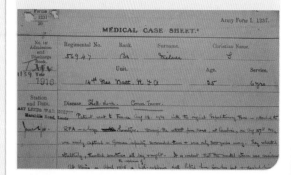

Personal accounts

➕ Usually honest – diaries are written just for the author and letters are to loved ones (but some know theirs may be published).

➕ Can give useful information and opinions on someone's experiences.

➖ Only give one individual's view and that person may not remember things clearly.

➖ Letters were censored and writers may want to protect loved ones.

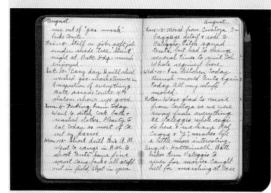

Newspapers

➕ Can give the 'big picture' of events or trends and show what the British public knew.

➕ Usually contain accurate facts such as numbers and statistics.

➖ All were censored during the war – so only give government-approved information.

➖ Purpose is to sell newspapers so only the 'best' stories are chosen.

GREAT BRITAIN DECLARES WAR ON GERMANY.

SUMMARY REJECTION OF BRITISH ULTIMATUM.

Photographs

➕ Usually factually accurate –difficult to 'stage' a photograph during battle.

➕ Can really help viewers see what it was like (though only black and white).

➖ Only shows a specific view at a particular time and place.

➖ Photographer may work for someone and has chosen to take that photo.

FRAMING QUESTIONS AND SELECTING SOURCES

In question 2(b), you will need to be able to frame a suitable question and select appropriate sources to follow up a detail in the source provided.

Framing of questions

Any source will leave the reader with unanswered questions or information that they want to follow up.

- You must pick a detail from the source – either something you can see in an image or a written detail in a text source – and describe that detail.
- Use this detail to write a question to be investigated. It must relate to the detail – so if the detail is about infections, then the question needs to be directly relevant to this.

Selection of sources

Once you have decided on a question, you need to think of a source that would help you to answer this question. Your knowledge of the strengths and weaknesses of different sources will help with this (see **page 55**). For example:

- If your question is about a medical technique, then a medical source, such as hospital records or medical journals, is likely to be a good one. Sources written by patients are unlikely to be as good as those written by people carrying out medical treatments.
- If your question is on the experiences of people in a specific role, then personal accounts, such as letters or diaries written by people in that role would help with your enquiry.

1. How useful are Sources B and C for an enquiry into the conditions in the trenches?

   Explain your answer using Sources B and C and your knowledge of the historical context. [8]

2. How could you follow up Source C to find out more about ill health in the trenches? [4]

1. *Your answer may include:*

Source B

- *Source B is very useful for this enquiry because it is an actual soldier's testimony of his first experiences in the trenches and includes details on what the trenches were like.*
- *Phrases like 'sloshed down' shows that the trenches could be very muddy and wet.*
- *It also gives information on the different types of trench and describes how the frontline trench was the most dangerous place to be as soldiers could be shot by enemy fire.*
- *The testimony was recorded after the war so some details may not be accurate.*
- *However much of what he says is supported by my own knowledge which indicates that this source is reliable. The trenches could get very waterlogged and muddy, especially during bad weather. Frontline trenches were indeed the most dangerous of the trenches as they were within range of enemy guns and artillery.*

Source C

- *Source C is useful because it is a photograph from the First World War showing soldiers standing in water surrounding by mud.*
- *It is unlikely that this photograph was staged so I think that it is an accurate portrayal of what conditions in the trenches were like.*
- *The photo is less useful because it only gives one view of the trench, and it looks like it has been posed because the men are looking directly at the camera. We also don't know who took the photo and what the photo was used for.*
- *However, the photo agrees with my knowledge that the trenches were filthy and often flooded, and the barbed wire supports my research that the trenches were protected by barbed wire.*

This question should be marked in accordance with the levels-based mark scheme on page 65.

2. **Detail in Source C that I would follow up:** *The flooding in the trenches.*[1]

   Question I would ask: *How did flooding in the trenches affect the health of soldiers?*[1]

   What type of source I could use: *Army records of battalions serving in the trenches on the Western Front.*[1]

   How this might help answer my question: *They would contain reports on the condition of the trenches and impacts on the soldiers' health.*[1]

Make sure your answers are in full sentences. Bullet points have been used in this example answer to suggest some information you could include.

EXAMINATION PRACTICE

1. Describe **two** features of problems caused by the terrain for medical treatment on the Western Front. [4]

2. (a) Study Source A and Source B. How useful are Sources A and B for an enquiry into new techniques in the treatment of wounds and infections on the Western Front?

    Explain your answer, using Sources A and B and your knowledge of the historical context. [8]

> **Source A:**
>
> **An extract from an article in the British Medical Journal by a surgeon, 1917. He describes the results of blood transfusion when used on cases of very serious blood loss and shock on the Western Front in 1917.**
>
> *The results have shown:*
>
> 1. *Certain patients previously considered inoperable, and others that needed exceedingly risky surgery, may often be revived to a certain degree which not only allows operations to take place, but also ensures a good prospect of ultimate recovery.*
>
> 2. *In other cases where the patient is on the verge of shock due to blood loss and the severity of the operation, blood transfusion is a permanent resuscitative measure of extreme value.*

> **Source B:**
>
> Medical staff at a base hospital use a Thomas splint to treat a patient with a broken leg.

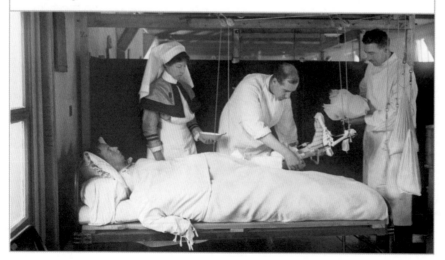

(b) Study Source A. How could you follow up Source A to find out more about new techniques in the treatment of patients on the Western Front?

In your answer, you must give the question you would ask and the type of source you could use.

Complete the table below. [4]

Detail in Source A that I would follow up:	
Question I would ask:	
What type of source I could use:	
How this might help answer my question:	

EXAMINATION PRACTICE ANSWERS

Section B has been covered before Section A to provide a greater background to Key Topic 5 - the Historic Environment.

Section B

1.   Your answer may include: [4]

In the medieval period, physicians used urine charts to diagnose disease. They would compare their patient's urine to a chart to check its appearance, smell, and even taste. This is different from the renaissance period when doctors began observing and recording their patient's symptoms to help them diagnose patients. This was largely thanks to the work of the doctor, Thomas Sydenham, who stressed the importance of a scientific approach when diagnosing patients.

2.   Your answer may include: [12]

A significant reason why medical treatments were largely ineffective during this period is because not enough was known about the causes of disease. For centuries, people incorrectly believed that disease was caused by imbalanced humours, and this could be cured using the theory of opposites. This theory suggested that a patient could be treated by giving them something to eat or drink which was opposite to their symptoms. For example, if a patient had a fever, they might be given cucumber to cool them down. Because the theory of the four humours was so widely accepted, most people didn't look for alternative treatments. We know now that imbalanced humours do not cause illness, so the theory of opposites was ineffective.

Bloodletting was another ineffective medieval treatment used to balance the four humours. Again, this treatment was ineffective because illness is not caused by an imbalance of the humours. As well as being ineffective, bloodletting could also be dangerous because it could weaken the patient.

Furthermore, since most people in the medieval period believed that illness was a punishment from God, many treatments for disease and illness were also centred around religion. People believed that prayer, fasting and giving offerings to the church would help cure them. Because so many people believed that God could cure them, they didn't look for alternative, rational treatments that may have been more effective.

Another reason why medical treatments in the period 1250–1500 were largely ineffective is because the Church had a lot of control over medicine. The Church banned dissections which meant that physicians couldn't study the human body to understand what caused disease, and therefore how to treat it. Physicians were also taught the Church's belief that the work of Galen and Hippocrates were universally correct, so they needn't look for other explanations for the causes of disease or ways to treat patients.

3.   Your answer may include: [16 + 4]

The introduction of the 1875 Public Health Act made huge strides towards reducing infectious diseases by improving clean water supplies, sanitation and housing. However, there were other factors that played a more significant role in preventing illness. The Act saw the employment of health officers and sanitary inspectors which ensured that public health provision would continue to be enforced and standards would be maintained. These actions led to a reduction in the diseases which are spread by microbes. For example, there were no cholera epidemics after 1866, and the Public Health Act probably contributed to this. As well as reducing the impact of infectious diseases, the Public Health Act helped to increase life expectancy. Thanks to the success of the Public Health Act, people were more willing to support government intervention in other health matters which would lead to further improvements in preventing disease.

However, the work of individuals also helped to prevent disease in this period. Louis Pasteur's Germ Theory suggested that specific microbes caused disease which led to him, and others, developing vaccines to prevent diseases such as anthrax and rabies. The introduction of these vaccines meant that it was possible to prevent people from catching or dying from specific diseases very effectively.

Knowledge and acceptance of Germ Theory, as well as the work of individuals such as Florence Nightingale and Joseph Lister, led to much cleaner surroundings in hospitals and during surgery. This helped to change people's attitudes towards antiseptic and aseptic environments. By 1900, surgeons wore protective surgical outfits, instruments were steam-cleaned, and hospitals segregated the infectious and had better ventilation and clean water supplies. This helped to prevent patients from catching infectious diseases during surgery and while receiving hospital care.

Furthermore, governments have played a significant role in preventing diseases beyond the Public Health Act. The development of vaccines in the later 19th century led to government vaccination campaigns such as polio and diphtheria which helped to dramatically reduce the number of people contracting these diseases and led to the almost total eradication of polio by the 1970s.

Government lifestyle campaigns in the twentieth and twenty-first centuries, such as 'five a day' and 'stop smoking', have helped to prevent disease through education and awareness. The government have taken further steps against lung cancer where 79% of cases are preventable. They have banned smoking in public places and made it illegal to advertise tobacco products.

In conclusion, although the Public Health Act was a significant factor in preventing illness during this period, I believe that other government involvement, namely the introduction of vaccination campaigns was more significant because they not only saved the lives of millions, but also contributed to the eradication of several fatal diseases, such as smallpox.

4. Your answer may include: [16 + 4]

To some extent I agree that there was little progress in medical treatment in Britain in 1500–1900. Many physicians still used ancient and ineffective treatments such as bloodletting throughout this period. Although it was less common, some physicians practised these treatments well into the 19th century.

The discoveries of the renaissance did not improve understanding of the cause of disease so there was little progress in the treatment of disease. For example, William Harvey improved knowledge of circulation and Vesalius improved knowledge of human anatomy but these individuals did not improve knowledge of illnesses or how to treat them.

Another reason why there was little progress is because many people could not afford access to proper healthcare. Most illnesses continued to be treated in the home by untrained people using herbal remedies from homemade recipes or apothecaries and later, medicines bought from quack doctors. By 1900 only a few people could afford access to a physician, so there was little progress in treatment because most people didn't have the money to pay for treatments.

It was not until after 1850 that people began to gradually understand the cause of some diseases. By 1900, due to the work of scientists such as Pasteur and Koch, most people accepted that germs caused illnesses. However, it would still take many years for this knowledge to lead to successful treatments for disease.

Although there was limited progress in this period, some medical treatments did improve. Hospital treatment changed greatly between 1500 and 1900. In 1500, hospitals were used as places for travellers to stay as well as for people to recuperate from illness, and few medical treatments were offered. However, by 1900, hospitals offered a far greater range of medical treatments, including complex surgery.

Furthermore, in 1500, most care in hospitals was given by monks and nuns who were not medically trained, and most treatments revolved around religion, such as prayer. By 1900, care and treatments in hospitals was given by trained doctors and surgeons and, due to the influence of Florence Nightingale, increasingly by trained nurses.

Before the 1850s, surgery was rare and was confined to mostly removing limbs, but improvements in anaesthetics, such as the discovery of chloroform in 1847, meant that surgeons could work more slowly and could carry out more complex surgery. The discovery of antiseptics, such as carbolic acid in 1865, helped to prevent infection and dramatically increased the chances of surviving surgery. This meant that by 1900, surgical treatment was far more common, more complex and more successful than in 1500.

In conclusion, although some elements of medical treatment saw limited progress in this period, I believe that surgery and hospital care saw massive improvements, thanks to the introduction of anaesthetics, antiseptics and better training for surgeons doctors and nurses.

Section A

1. Your answer may include: [4]

Holes and craters in the ground caused by shells as well as deep mud or even snow made transport very difficult. Ambulances could not get through and stretcher bearers took a long time to get the wounded to medical help. The bumpy and uneven terrain meant that patients were jostled and moved around when they were carried on stretcher or by ambulance. This could cause further injury and increase blood loss which lowered patients' chances of survival.

2. (a)   Your answer may include: [8]

Source A
The following points could be made about the source's content:

Detail on how blood transfusions revive patients so that surgery can be carried out is useful because it shows that this new technique was helping patients who were not being helped before.

Detail on how blood transfusions were successfully helping patients who had lost blood during and after operations is useful because it shows another way in which this new technique helped patients survive.

Detail on how blood transfusions are improving patients' chances of recovery is useful as it shows the success of this procedure.

The following points could be made about the source's provenance:

The author is a surgeon who was carrying out this procedure on the Western Front which suggests this source is accurate and confirms that it is useful.

The fact that this is from an article in a medical journal suggests that it is accurate and gives important information as other medical professionals would be reading it.

The author may want to exaggerate the success of the treatments to gain more publicity for himself.

Knowledge of the historical context could be used to support and assess the usefulness of the sources:

Blood loss was a huge problem on the Western Front and led to many deaths – blast injuries and gunshot wounds both caused blood loss, and transportation over bumpy ground by stretcher, horse-drawn or motor ambulance often increased blood loss.

Blood transfusions were rarely carried out before 1917 as only person-to-person transfusions could be done and it was difficult to do this during warfare.

Bruce Robertson was a pioneer of indirect blood transfusions and helped prove their effectiveness – many British medics believed that saline injections were as effective as transfusing blood before his work.

Source B

The following points could be made about the source's content:

Image shows a patient being treated with a Thomas splint which is useful because this was a new method for treating broken legs which was introduced from 1916.

The image is useful because it shows a Thomas splint in place which aids understanding of how it was attached to the patient.

The image is less useful because the image gives no indication of how the splint is helping the patient to recover.

The following points could be drawn from the source's provenance:

There is no information on who the photographer is or why they were taking this image which might make it less useful as we don't know the purpose of the source, but it might have been taken to reassure people that soldiers were receiving good care, or to demonstrate the work being done by medical professionals.

The photograph was probably posed, as the photographer would have needed permission to take the photo.

Knowledge of the historical context could be used to support and assess the usefulness of the sources:

Broken legs were a serious problem on the Western Front as they had a very high mortality rate. The introduction of the Thomas splint from 1916 helped increase survival rates.

Base hospitals treated patients who could not be treated at Casualty Clearing Stations, or who needed more time to recuperate from their injuries as would be the case with broken legs.

Base hospitals had better equipment and more specialised medical personnel than other stages of treatment. They also had plenty of beds which allowed injured soldiers to recover.

(b) Your answer may include: [4]

Detail in Source A that I would follow up: Some patients were not treated due to blood loss that made them unlikely to survive – 'Certain patients previously considered inoperable'.

Question I would ask: How often were patients considered inoperable because they had lost too much blood?

What type of source I could use: RAMC medical records of patients who were not operated on.

How this might help answer my question: The records would record the injuries of patients, including blood loss and why they were not treated.

LEVELS-BASED MARK SCHEMES FOR EXTENDED RESPONSE QUESTIONS

Questions 2(a), 3, 4 and 5/6 require extended writing and use mark bands. Each answer will be assessed against the mark bands, and a mark is awarded based on the mark band it fits into.

The descriptors have been written in simple language to give an indication of the expectations of each mark band. See the Edexcel website for the official mark schemes used.

Question 2 (a)

Level 3 (6–8 marks)	• The answer gives a judgement on usefulness for the specific enquiry with valid criteria and developed reasoning. • The answer assesses the impact of content and provenance on usefulness. • The sources are analysed to support the argument. • The answer demonstrates contextual knowledge to interpret sources and assess usefulness.
Level 2 (3–5 marks)	• The answer gives a judgement on usefulness for the specific enquiry with valid criteria. • The answer assesses content and provenance. • There is some analysis of sources through selecting material to support the argument. • The answer demonstrates contextual knowledge to support comments on content and/or provenance
Level 1 (1–2 marks)	• The answer gives a simple judgement on usefulness. • The answer gives undeveloped reasoning on content and/or provenance. • There is simple understanding of the sources and content is repeated. • The answer demonstrates limited contextual knowledge.
0 marks	• No answer has been given or the answer given makes no relevant points.

Question 3

Level 3 (3–4 marks)	• The answer analyses features of the period(s) to explain a similarity/difference. • The answer includes specific supporting information which shows good knowledge and understanding of the period(s).
Level 2 (1–2 marks)	• The answer offers a simple or generalised comment about a similarity/difference. • The answer includes generalised information about the topic which shows limited knowledge and understanding of the period(s).
0 marks	• No answer has been given or the answer given makes no relevant points.

Question 4

Level 4 (10–12 marks)	• The answer gives an analytical explanation which is focused on the question. • The answer is well developed, coherent and logically structured. • The information given is accurate and relevant to the question. • The answer shows excellent knowledge and understanding of the topic. • The answer includes information that goes beyond the stimulus points in the question.
Level 3 (7–9 marks)	• The answer shows some analysis which is generally focused on the question. • The answer is mostly coherent and logically structured. • Most of the information given is accurate and relevant to the question. • The answer shows good knowledge and understanding of the topic.
Level 2 (4–6 marks)	• The answer shows limited analysis, and not all points are justified. • The answer shows some organisation, but the reasoning is not sustained. • Some accurate and relevant information is given. • The answer shows some knowledge and understanding of the topic.
Level 1 (1–3 marks)	• A simple or general answer is given. • The answer lacks development or organisation. • The answer shows limited knowledge and understanding of the topic.
0 marks	• No answer has been given or the answer given makes no relevant points.

Question 5 and 6 – SPaG (Spelling, Punctuation and Grammar)

High 4 marks	• The answer uses consistent spelling and punctuation. • The answer uses grammar correctly and effectively. • The answer includes a wide range of specialist terms, where appropriate.
Intermediate 2–3 marks	• The answer largely uses consistent spelling and punctuation. • The answer uses grammar correctly. • The answer includes a good range of specialist terms, where appropriate.
Threshold 1 mark	• The answer shows a reasonable level of correct spelling and punctuation. • The answer shows some control of grammar, and errors do not hinder meaning. • The answer includes a limited range of specialist terms, where appropriate.
0 marks	• No answer is given, or the answer does not relate to the question. • The answer does not meet the threshold performance level, and errors severely hinder meaning.

Question 5 and 6 – Content

Level 4 (13–16 marks)	• The answer gives an explanation with analysis which is consistently focussed on the question. • The answer is well reasoned with supporting evidence, and it is clear and well organised. • The answer includes accurate and relevant information that has been appropriately selected to answer the question directly. • The answer shows broad knowledge and clear understanding of the topic. • The answer reaches a well-supported and clear judgement. • The answer includes information that goes beyond what has been mentioned in the stimulus points.
Level 3 (9–12 marks)	• The answer gives an explanation with some analysis which is largely focused on the question. • The answer is fairly well reasoned with supporting evidence, but it may lack some clarity and organisation. • The answer includes accurate and relevant information, with good knowledge and understanding of the topic. • The answer gives an overall judgement with some justification, but some supporting evidence is only implied or not correctly used.
Level 2 (5–8 marks)	• The answer shows limited or unsupported analysis of the question. • There is limited development and organisation, and the reasoning is not sustained. • The answer includes some accurate and relevant information, that shows some knowledge of the topic. • The answer gives an overall judgement, but it is not fully justified, or the justification is weak.
Level 1 (1–4 marks)	• A simple answer is given, which lacks development and organisation. • The answer shows limited knowledge and understanding of the topic. • The answer doesn't provide an overall judgement.
0 marks	• No answer has been given or the answer given makes no relevant points.

INDEX

MEDICINE TIMELINE

This timeline highlights some of the most important medical developments, discoveries, and events during c1250–present.

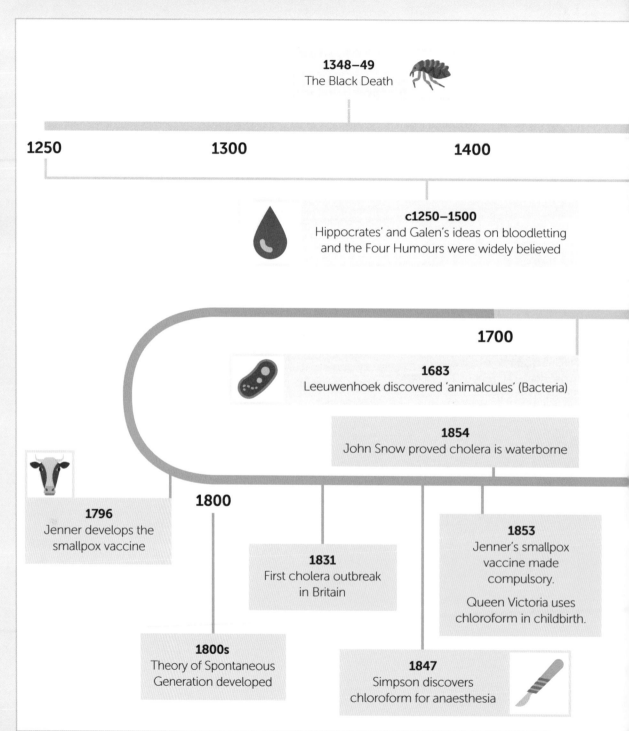

1348–49
The Black Death

1250   1300   1400

c1250–1500
Hippocrates' and Galen's ideas on bloodletting and the Four Humours were widely believed

1700

1683
Leeuwenhoek discovered 'animalcules' (Bacteria)

1854
John Snow proved cholera is waterborne

1800

1796
Jenner develops the smallpox vaccine

1853
Jenner's smallpox vaccine made compulsory.

Queen Victoria uses chloroform in childbirth.

1831
First cholera outbreak in Britain

1800s
Theory of Spontaneous Generation developed

1847
Simpson discovers chloroform for anaesthesia

c1470
Printing press
developed in Europe

1500

c1500
Around 1,300
hospitals in operation

16th C
English Reformation. The Church
had less control over what
physicians were taught, but there
was a decline in hospitals

1600s
Royal Touch
ceremonies
peaked in
popularity

1600

1665
Great Plague of London

1628
Harvey published
ideas on circulation

Early 1600s
Microscope invented

1861
Pasteur published Germ Theory

1898
Viruses discovered

1929
Fleming discovers penicillin

1900

1895
X-ray machines developed

1930s
DNA discovered

1875
Public Health Act passed

1932
Second magic bullet,
Prontosil, developed

1865
Lister developed antiseptic
surgery with carbolic acid

1906
First magic bullet,
Salvasan, developed

1948
NHS introduced

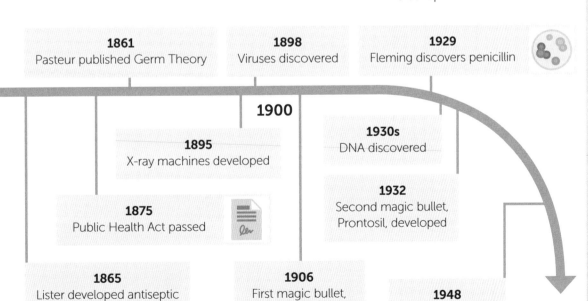

ACKNOWLEDGEMENTS

The questions in the ClearRevise textbook are the sole responsibility of the authors and have neither been provided nor approved by the examination board.

Every effort has been made to trace and acknowledge ownership of copyright. The publishers will be happy to make any future amendments with copyright owners that it has not been possible to contact. The publisher would like to thank the following companies and individuals who granted permission for the use of their images and extracts in this textbook.

All graphics and images not mentioned below © Shutterstock

Image on p7	–	St. Bartholomew's. Wellcome Collection. Attribution 4.0 International (CC BY 4.0)
Image on p9	–	Black Death in Tournai © Pictorial Press Ltd / Alamy Stock Photo
Image on p11	–	Thomas Sydenham painting © GRANGER – Historical Picture Archive / Alamy Stock Photo
Image on p11	–	Llyfrgell Genedlaethol Cymru – The National Library of Wales
Image on p13	–	Queen Mary I Curing Subject with Royal Touch © Alamy Stock Photo
Image on p14	–	'Here you may be cured!' - a 17th century quack doctor © Alamy Stock Photo
Image on p15	–	A learned physician with a library of Latin books writes a prescription but cannot save his patients from death. Etching by G.M. Mitelli, c. 1700. Wellcome Collection.
Image on p16	–	Two figures with their thoracic cavity exposed, one dissecting the other (figs I-II), together with illustrations mainly of the heart (figs III-XI) and two of the lungs (figs XII-XIII). Engraving, 1568. Wellcome Collection.
Image on p17	–	A street during the plague in London with a death cart and mourners. Colour wood engraving by E. Evans. Wellcome Collection.
Image on p23	–	Sir J. Y. Simpson and two friends, having tested chloroform on themselves, lying insensible on the floor around a table. Pen and ink drawing. Wellcome Collection.
Image on p24	–	Everett Collection Historical / Alamy Stock Photo © Everett Collection Historical / Alamy Stock Photo
Image on p25	–	Jenner Vaccinating Boy © Alamy Stock Photo
Image on p27	–	A woman dropping her porcelain tea-cup in horror upon discovering the monstrous contents of a magnified drop of Thames water; revealing the impurity of London drinking water. Coloured etching by W. Heath, 1828. Wellcome Collection.
Image on p28	–	A dead victim of cholera at Sunderland in 1832. Coloured lithograph attributed to J.W. Gear. Wellcome Collection.
Image on p28	–	Map of Soho from the UCLA Department of Epidemiology.
Image on p32	–	Tube of Prontosil tablets, Germany, 1935-1950. Science Museum, London. Attribution 4.0 International (CC BY 4.0)
Images on p33	–	A&E © Imran Khan / Shutterstock
		Boots Pharmacy © Alex Segre / Shutterstock
Image on p37	–	Sir Alexander Fleming (1881-1955) © Alamy Stock Photo
Image on p38	–	Sir Ernst Boris Chain, (1906 – 1979) © Alamy Stock Photo
Image on p38	–	Howard Walter Florey, (1898 – 1968) © Alamy Stock Photo
Image on p44	–	WWI Horse and cart © Everett Collection / Shutterstock
Image on p45	–	Soldiers © Everett Collection / Shutterstock
Image on p46	–	© Imperial War Museum (Q 10622)
Image on p48	–	First Aid Nursing Yeomanry Corps 1914 © Alamy Stock Photo
Image on p50	–	World War I: British army operating theatre near Boulogne. Wellcome Collection. Attribution 4.0 International (CC BY 4.0)
Image on p51	–	Blood transfusion between two people, J. Roussel, 1876. © Alamy Stock Photo
Image on p52	–	A British soldier with bandaged head © Alamy Stock Photo
Image on p53	–	Thomas-type leg splint, Europe, 1901-1920. Science Museum, London. Attribution 4.0 International (CC BY 4.0)
Image on p53	–	Blood transfusion apparatus, United Kingdom, 1914-1918. Science Museum, London. Attribution 4.0 International (CC BY 4.0)
Image on p54	–	First World War discharge certificate © Alamy Stock Photo
Image on p54	–	Reverse of WW1 era postcard © Alamy Stock Photo
Image on p55	–	World War I: operating theatre in H.M.S. Burbis. Wellcome Collection. Attribution 4.0 International (CC BY 4.0)
Image on p56	–	Hospital records from the National Archives. Reproduced under the Open Government Licence v3.0
Image on p56	–	World War I: transport of wounded in ambulance. Wellcome Collection. Attribution 4.0 International (CC BY 4.0)
Image on p56	–	Britain declares war on Germany, 1914 © Alamy Stock Photo
Extract on p58	–	© Imperial War Museum (sound file 11440 (quote from reel 3))
Image on p58	–	Two British soldiers stand in a flooded communications trench on the Western Front 1917 © Alamy Stock Photo
Extract on p60	–	Copyright © 1917, BMJ Publishing Group Ltd
Image on p60	–	© Imperial War Museum (Q 33472)

EXAMINATION TIPS

With your examination practice, use a boundary approximation using the following table. These boundaries have been calculated as an average across all past History papers rather than an average of this paper. Be aware that boundaries are usually a few percentage points either side of this. They shroud be used as a guideline only.

Grade	9	8	7	6	5	4	3	2	1
Boundary	83%	75%	67%	58%	51%	42%	30%	19%	8%

1. Make sure your handwriting is legible. The examiner can't award you marks if they can't read what you've written.

2. Read the questions carefully. Don't give an answer to a question that you think is appearing (or wish was appearing!) rather than the actual question.

3. In Q2(b) you'll be asked about one of two sources. Make sure you write about the source specified in the question. If you write about the wrong source, you won't get any marks, no matter how good your answer is.

4. Don't spend too long on Q1, 2(b) and 3 as they're only worth 4 marks each. Make sure you've left yourself plenty of time to answer Q4 and 5/6 since they're worth 12 and 20 marks.

5. For the Thematic Study, make sure you know exactly which time period you are being asked about and if it has an alternative name (medieval period, renaissance etc). Remember that the 19th century refers to the 1800s, not the 1900s!

6. To get top marks in Q4 and 5/6, you need to include information beyond what is provided in the bullet points. Jotting down a quick plan before you start can help make sure your answer includes sufficient detail and is focused on the question.

7. Your answers to Q4 and 5/6 need to show breadth, i.e. include examples from across the time period you've been asked about.

8. In the longer written questions, use linking words and phrases to show you are developing your points or comparing information, for example, "as a consequence", "this shows that" and "on the other hand". This helps to give your answer structure, and makes it easier for the examiner to award you marks.

9. Your answer to Q5/6 will be marked for correct spelling, punctuation and grammar, as well as using topic-specific vocabulary correctly. Don't throw away marks by using casual language, poor spelling and no paragraphs.

10. If you need extra paper, make sure you clearly signal that your answer is continued elsewhere. Remember that longer answers don't necessarily score more highly than shorter, more concise answers.

Good luck!

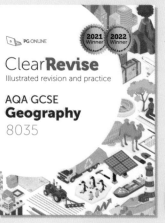

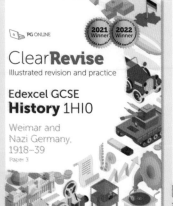